Nubia: A Drowning Land

Margaret Drower

Paintings by Alan Sorrell

Longmans

LONGMANS YOUNG BOOKS LIMITED
LONDON AND HARLOW

Associated companies, branches and representatives throughout the world.

SBN: 582 16440 0

ACKNOWLEDGEMENTS

The publishers gratefully acknowledge permission to use the following illustrations in this book: K. Michalowski, Faras-Expedition, Photo Gerster-Rapho for the photograph on page 72; The Egypt Exploration Society for the illustration reproduced from *The Tomb of Huy* on page 38; Vattenbyggnadsbyran (VBB), Stockholm, for the chart on pages 54-5.

All the remaining pictures in the book are by Alan Sorrell. The illustrations on pages 15, 29, and 66 are reconstructions and the publishers wish to thank the *Illustrated London News* for permission to reproduce the reconstruction on page 29. The publishers also wish to thank the *Illustrated London News* for permission to reproduce the paintings on pages 10, 11, 25, 27, 28, 32, 40, 42, 44, 45, 46, 47, 49, 50-1, 52, 53, 60, 67, 69, 74, 75, 76, 78, 79, 80, 81, and 83.

Printed in Great Britain by
W. S. Cowell Ltd, at the Butter Market, Ipswich

Foreword

This is the story of a land under sentence of death. By the autumn of 1969, when the High Dam is finished, Nubia will no longer exist. Already it has almost disappeared under an ever-widening lake, as the waters of the Nile pile up behind the great barrier which will, it is hoped, bring sustenance to millions in Egypt. For those who have known and loved the country, it is difficult to speak of it in the past tense, for the memory of its harsh beauty, the sunlight, the silence and the empty, rocky spaces will always be vividly present.

We have tried in this book to paint a portrait of Nubia in words and pictures, and to outline, very briefly, its history. In doing so, we have also told another story, that of a great international campaign, undertaken when the fateful decision to build the dam had been made, and it became inevitable that what the Nile had given, the Nile would destroy.

Alan Sorrell, commissioned by Sir Bruce Ingram, the Editor of the *Illustrated London News*, to make drawings of the sites and landscapes about to be destroyed, travelled about Nubia in February and March, 1962, when the campaign 'Save the Monuments of Nubia' had already begun. His journey to Abu Simbel and back was made in an 84-foot launch, the *Sheikh el Beled*, put at his disposal by the Government of the United Arab Republic through the initiative and kindness of H. E. Dr Sarwat Okasha, Minister of Culture and National Guidance. While at Abu Simbel, he stayed on board the house-boat *Hathor* as the guest of the Government Documentation Centre. His warm thanks go to Mr Abdin Siam, Inspector of Nubian Antiquities, who acted as guide and interpreter, to the Sudan Department of Antiquities for assistance and transport, to Professor Kelly Simpson at whose camp he stayed at Arminna, and to Professor W. B. Emery and Mrs Emery for help and hospitality at the Egypt Exploration Society's camp in Buhen. The *Illustrated London News* published a selection of the drawings from June 1962 to April 1963, and the complete collection was shown in London at a reception given by H. E. Muhamed el Kony, Ambassador of the United Arab Republic. The collection was purchased in 1968 by Mr F. D. Todman, and through his generosity is now on permanent loan to the Beecroft Art Gallery at Southend-on-Sea.

The writer, whose thanks are due to the Ministry of Tourism of the United Arab Republic for information and help, visited ancient sites in Nubia, from Philae to Semna in the Sudan, during the winters of 1961, 1962 and 1963 and assisted in one of the expeditions to excavate a doomed site and record a temple before its removal. Anyone who has had the good fortune to participate, as we have done, in the campaign of rescue has a sense of becoming personally involved. The need of a nation is a human claim which none can reject; but the loss of Nubia is a heavy price to pay.

June 1969   Margaret Drower

THE TEMPLE OF PTAH AT GERF HUSEIN. All that is left of the pillared hall. The dumpy columns and squat, clumsy figure of King Ramesses suggest local workmanship and are in sad contrast to the mastery of the sculptors at Abu Simbel. (See Chapter V.)

Contents

The Nile Valley

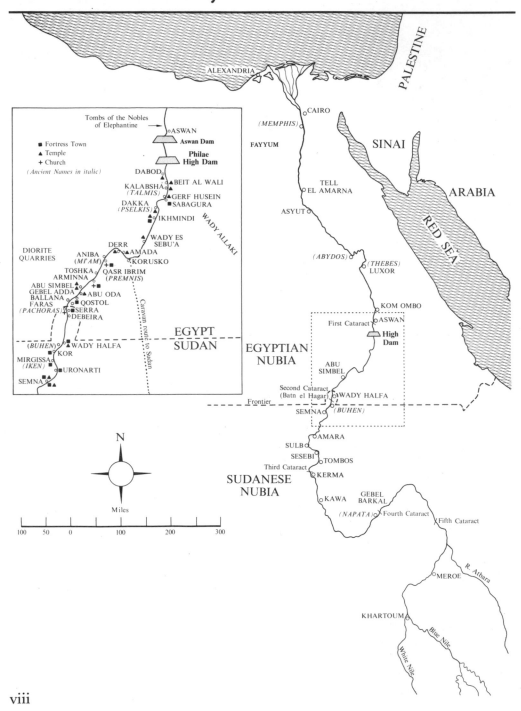

Historical Chart

Approximate Date	EGYPT		NUBIA
3000 BC	Archaic Period	1st and 2nd Dynasties	'A-Group' settlements. Military campaigns of King Djer and his successors.
2800	OLD KINGDOM	3rd to 6th Dynasties	Egyptian mining outposts at Buhen, Second Cataract region. Trading expeditions from Elephantine to the far south.
2200	First Intermediate Period	7th to 10th Dynasties	'C-Group' settlements.
2040	MIDDLE KINGDOM	11th to 13th Dynasties	Egyptians establish military control over Nubia. Fortification of Second Cataract region. Trading post at Kerma.
1730	Second Intermediate Period	14th and 17th Dynasties	Fortresses destroyed.
	Hyksos in Lower Egypt	15th and 16th Dynasties	Nubia an independent kingdom under the Prince of Kush.
1570	NEW KINGDOM	18th to 20th Dynasties	Reconquest of Nubia and annexation of Kush to beyond the Fourth Cataract. Rule of the Viceroys of Kush.
1290			Ramesses II builds temples.
1090	LATE PERIOD	21st to 30th Dynasties	Nubia again independent of Egypt. Kings of Kush at Napata.
730	Nubia and Egypt united under the 25th Dynasty		Conquest of Egypt by Piankhy.
525	Egypt a Persian province		
332	Alexander the Great conquers Egypt		Meroitic rulers in Napata, then in Meroe.
	PTOLEMAIC PERIOD		
30	Egypt becomes a Roman province		Nobatae and Blemmyes. 'X-Group' cemeteries.
AD 324	BYZANTINE PERIOD		
543			Conversion of Nubia to Christianity

EARLY MORNING AT DABOD. The east bank of the Nile.

DESERT LANDSCAPE AT TUMÂS. Beyond the houses, the desert stretches away with its strange, eroded rock pinnacles.

x

Introduction

The land of Nubia now belongs partly to Egypt and partly to the Sudan; it is the corridor that links them, the No Man's Land that divides them. In this section of its long winding course towards the Mediterranean, the Nile is confined in a narrow valley bounded on either side by the desert, a desert so desolate that no motor road or railway has ever yet been built there: to travel from Shellal at the First Cataract* to the town of Wady Halfa at the Second it has always been necessary to take to the river. Until a few years ago tourist steamers and government launches plied between the two. The journey took three days going upstream and, by fast steamer, thirty-six hours in the opposite direction. The villagers, watching the boats pass, remained untouched by the sophisticated world they represented.

* Below Khartoum, the Nile is interrupted by six cataracts, unnavigable stretches of rushing water; the first and most northerly is near Aswan.

The political boundary between Egypt and the Sudan now bisects the valley approximately on the 22nd parallel, at Adindan a little north of Wady Halfa. The northern half, Lower Nubia or Egyptian Nubia, was called in ancient times Wawat, while Upper Nubia, or Sudanese Nubia, was the land of Kush. The two regions were divided by the fifty-mile stretch of broken water, rocks and islands, nowadays called in Arabic *Batn el-Hagar*, 'Belly of Stones', that constitutes the Second Cataract.

Nubia is a harsh, inhospitable land. Rain falls very rarely, sometimes not once in ten years. For several months in the summer the thermometer reaches 120° or even 130° Fahrenheit; the sun blazes down from a cloudless sky and every bush and tree becomes an oasis of shade and rest. Occasional deposits of silt by the river permit a little cultivation, a small patch of emerald green barley or a grove of date palms. As one travels upstream, the land assumes bizarre shapes: the eye is caught by strange natural formations like pyramids, or conical coal-tips. On the west bank, a waste of rock and wind-blown sand stretches away across the Sahara to the Atlantic Ocean, a thousand miles away. Between Kalabsha and Gerf Husein, the Tropic of Cancer is crossed; by night the stars shine brilliantly and, low on the horizon, the Southern Cross is visible – another reminder that Nubia stretches out towards the heart of Africa.

Both by reason of its poverty and also because of its geographical position, the destinies of Nubia have always been closely linked with those of Egypt. To the ancient Egyptians, Nubia was a land to be coveted and, if possible, conquered. It was 'The Land of Bowmen', fighting tribes who might at any time threaten the security of their southern frontier; it was the way to the untold wealth of inner Africa. When strong kings sat on the Egyptian throne, they ruled Nubia, exploiting its mineral wealth and carrying off cattle and slaves; in time of weakness, control was lost and the Nubians for a time went their own way, only to be reconquered as a new warrior dynasty arose at Thebes. The history of ancient Nubia is therefore the story of the ancient Egyptians and must be narrated along with the rising and falling fortunes of that people.

A very brief summary of Egyptian history may here be of use, since it explains several terms and concepts which occur frequently in this book.*

* The reader is referred also to the chronological chart on p. ix, where the parallel course of Egyptian and Nubian history is tabulated.

2

The history of Egypt during the time of the Pharaohs (the pharaonic period) was divided in antiquity into thirty-one dynasties, each representing a royal family or group of kings originating from a particular locality. A change of dynasty often meant political upheaval of some sort resulting in the transfer of power to a new line. These divisions, hallowed by custom, are still retained by historians, in spite of their imperfections, as a convenient framework. A more significant scheme has been devised, however, in modern times, whereby pharaonic history is regarded as a succession of five main periods: the Archaic or Early Dynastic Period; the Old Kingdom (the age of the pyramid builders); the Middle Kingdom, in some ways the best period in art

THE TOWN OF BALLANA, near Abu Simbel. Donkeys cross the canal to the market (sûq); the minaret of a mosque is seen in the background.

and literature, and a time of military expansion; the New Kingdom, when Egypt became a leading world power and won an empire extending from the Sudan to the Euphrates; and the Late Period, a troubled time when the country again and again suffered invasion and foreign rule. Between the Old and the Middle Kingdoms, and between the Middle and the New, two Intermediate Periods are recognized, when the central authority collapsed and the country was divided between petty dynasts each claiming the royal titles.

At the close of the Pharaonic period, Alexander the Great conquered Egypt and founded the city of Alexandria. After his death, the government of the country was assigned to one of his generals, Ptolemy Lagus, who in 306 BC took the title of king as Ptolemy Soter. Under the Ptolemies, or Lagids (descendants of Lagus) as they are sometimes called, Egypt continued to prosper. Greeks and Egyptian lived side by side but the national character was not greatly affected and the old religion survived. The rule of the Ptolemaic dynasty lasted until, after the defeat of Anthony and Cleopatra at the battle of Actium, Egypt passed into the hands of Augustus. Henceforward Egypt was to be a Roman province, governed by a Prefect. The country was exploited for the benefit of the Roman emperors and drained of its resources; revolts and riots punctuate its turbulent history. The Christian faith took root early in Egypt and some of the disturbances were religious quarrels between rival sects. The monastic movement flourished, and monasteries proliferated.

In AD 639 the Arab conqueror, Amr ibn el Âs, captured Memphis and Egypt became a province of the Caliphate; Islam became the official faith but Christianity was tolerated. The Copts of today, though they now speak Arabic like the Moslem majority in the country, still retain in their liturgy the language of the ancient Egyptians, whose descendants they may be considered to be. We shall see presently that in Nubia, Christianity came later, but took a stronger hold.

Without the Nile, Nubia and Egypt would not exist. For more than six thousand years, those who have lived by the river have welcomed the annual rise of the flood water in summer, waited until it subsided and then planted their wheat and their barley in the soft black fertile silt, rich in minerals, which it deposited on the fields. As long ago as the time of the Pharaohs, men learned to extend the area of their fields by cutting ditches and canals so that

4

BY THE NILE AT MARIYA. In the foreground is a dismantled waterwheel. Farther away, a shadûf *or waterlift is being used to irrigate a tiny patch of maize.*

the Nile could spread its flow over ground a little distant from its banks. Along these canals and along the banks of the Nile, continuous irrigation was possible with the laborious aid of buckets, or, from about 1500 BC onwards, by means of the *shadûf* or bucket-lift; the animal-driven *sāgia*, the creaking water-wheel, was introduced in classical times, and during the last few decades only the petrol pump has made the farmer's task easier.

About 150 years ago, agriculture in Egypt underwent a transformation. The demand for cotton in the mills of Lancashire became urgent when, during the American Civil War, supplies from the southern states were cut off by blockade. In the 1880's, the British brought irrigation experts to Egypt from India, and a network of canals and barrages was built to enable the flood water to be conserved after the Nile subsided. By this new system, two cotton harvests a year became possible and the construction of the Aswan Dam between 1899 and 1902 enabled a huge volume of water to be stored. One hundred feet high, it could hold back 980,000,000 cubic feet of water. But this was not enough for Egypt's needs. The population was increasing rapidly and the economic demands of the country grew. The height of the dam was twice raised, so that the artificial lake expanded and the level of the Nile rose as far south as the Sudanese border. Only the heads of palm trees now showed above the water in wintertime, and the Nubian villagers, abandoning their houses at the base of the cliffs bordering the river, built new ones on the cliff top. In summer, when the river was low, they were able to cultivate their small plots in the valley.

But still the people of Egypt were in want, for the more prosperous the country became, the faster the population multiplied and increasing productivity could not keep pace. There was no lack of land: on either side of the narrow green ribbon of cultivation there are wide tracts of desert – all that was needed was water. And still the surplus waters of the Nile, which the Aswan Dam could not hold back, flowed away every year into the sea.

The decision was inevitable, and at last it was taken. A second and larger dam must be built, the High Dam (*Sadd el-Âli*). It was to be so large that it would hold back an immense volume of water, enough to provide for all Egypt's needs. So was initiated one of the greatest engineering projects ever planned by man, a project which is now nearing completion. Some miles south of the Aswan Dam, above Shellal the old railway terminus, a gigantic embankment has been constructed under the guidance of Russian engineers and technicians. It is nearly three miles long, and half a mile wide at the base. Upstream of it, the waters are held back so that the whole valley of the Nile is gradually filling to form a huge reservoir. The benefits expected from this scheme are enormous. Canals are being dug in the dry desert, so that new acres can be brought under cultivation. It is expected that an area almost half as large again as the present arable land can be claimed for tillage, so that with the aid of fertilizers the brown desert will become green fields. Also twelve giant turbines in the dam, with a total capacity of two million horse-power, will provide hydro-electric power, and industrial production in Egypt will be more than doubled.

But what of the land above the dam? Once the decision to build had been reached, a problem of terrifying urgency faced the planners. Within a few years, the geologists declared, the lake formed by the waters piled up behind the barrage would drown the whole of Nubia almost as far south as the Third Cataract, a distance of some three hundred miles. In places the new lake would spread out over the desert as far as the eye could see. Lake Nasser (as it is called) would submerge the villages and towns of Nubia; not only Aniba and Ballana in Egypt, but even the large town of Wady Halfa in the Sudan would disappear. The whole Nubian population would have to be moved to new homes elsewhere; the land itself, with its scores of ancient monuments, temples and medieval churches, the ruins of fortresses and ancient settlements, the cemeteries and all the other traces left by ancient man would be forever obliterated.

The same problem, on a much smaller scale, had faced the authorities when the first dam, the Aswan Dam, was heightened. In 1907 the first Archaeological Survey of Nubia was formed by the (then) Ministry of Public Works;

EXCAVATION IN PROGRESS AT ARMINNA. Traces of mudbrick walls have betrayed the presence of a Coptic house, which is being excavated by American archaeologists from Yale and Pennsylvania.

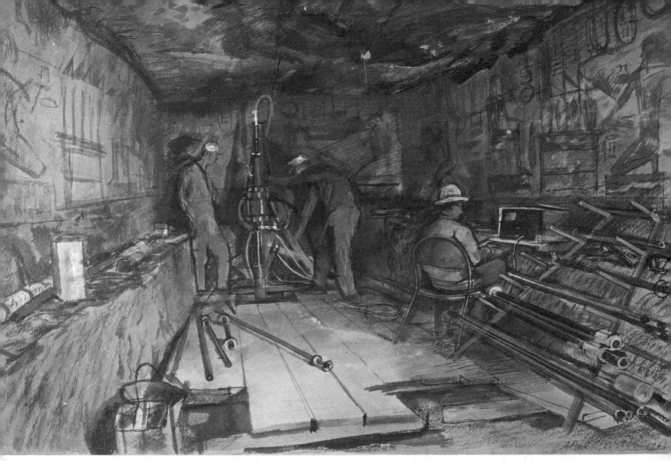

EXPERIMENTAL DRILLING AT ABU SIMBEL. Swedish engineers are testing the composition and friability of the rock in one of the store-chambers of the Great Temple. Upon their reports depended the decision to move the temple.

its direction was in the capable hands of an American archaeologist, George Reisner, and his excavations in 1907–8, aided by a team of British Egyptologists and a distinguished anthropologist, laid the foundations of modern Nubian archaeology. They concentrated on that part of the river valley which lay at a low level on either side of the Nile. The Second Archaeological survey, inaugurated by the Egyptian Antiquities Service in 1929 when the top of the Aswan Dam was to be raised for the second time, extended both survey and excavation to a higher level in the valley, and as far south as Adindan on the Sudanese border. This time it was directed by Walter Bryan Emery, now Professor of Egyptology in the University of London, and on his staff were a number of young Egyptian archaeologists. Some of the results of their work between 1929 and 1931 are mentioned in this book, the most spectacular being the finding of the royal tombs at Ballana and Qostol, described in Chapter VI.

The task imposed by the building of the High Dam, however, was too great for the governments of Egypt and the Sudan to tackle unaided. The cost of removing the most important of the stone monuments would be enormous; the burden of excavation and recording was beyond the capacity of any one or two expeditions, working against the clock. Accordingly, both countries appealed to the international body which had been set up after the Second World War for just this kind of emergency: the United Nations Educational, Scientific and Cultural Organization, or UNESCO. The responsibility for rescuing Nubia's past was to be that of the whole world. UNESCO undertook to launch a campaign to mobilize the financial and scientific resources of all nations and to summon the aid of learned societies, universities and governments throughout the world. It was a campaign unique in the annals of international co-operation. When the Director-General of UNESCO first launched his appeal, the French Minister of State for Culture, M. Malraux, said in Paris:

On this eighth of March, 1960, for the first time, the nations, though many of them are even now engaged in covert or open conflict, have been summoned to save by a united effort the fruits of civilization on which none has a pre-emptive claim. Such an appeal, in the last century, would have seemed fanciful. . . . Your appeal is historic, not because it proposes to save the temples of Nubia but because, through it, for the first time, world civilization publicly proclaims the world's art as its invisible heritage. In days when the West believed its cultural heritage had its source in Athens, it could nonetheless look on with equanimity while the Acropolis crumbled away . . .

More than forty nations offered help. Some sent monetary contributions; many offered practical aid. The whole doomed area of the Nubian Nile was parcelled up into a number of 'concessions', or areas of responsibility, and each concession was adopted by a different government mission or learned body. One or two missions assumed the task of surveying prehistoric remains on the upper Nile terraces, another the plotting of yet undiscovered cemeteries; anthropologists and sociologists undertook to study the Nubians in their villages, before their communities were broken up and the old customs and traditions forgotten. Their folklore, their art and their music, hitherto neglected, were to be studied and recorded. Each ancient monument was to be carefully planned, photographed and recorded by the expedition in whose

ANCIENT AND MODERN NUBIA. In the foreground, the ancient fort of Tumâs is under excavation. The mud houses of the villagers of today are not unlike those of their ancient forefathers.

territory it lay; the largest monuments were individually allotted to separate missions. Where possible facsimile copies were to be made of all relief sculpture, inscriptions and painted decoration. To do this various methods were available, the most usual being that of tracing the carving on the wall itself, or of making casts by means of latex moulds or of 'squeezes' (layers of wet paper pressed on to the surface of the relief and allowed to dry hard). A third method which has been extensively used in Nubia is photogrammetry; by this process stereoscopic photographs are taken which make a permanent record of the dimensions of an object and which can later be translated into exact replicas, accurate to a fiftieth of an inch. Once a complete record had been made, it was hoped to move most of the temples and other stone monuments to places of safety, and to re-erect them near the edge of the new lake. The preservation of these temples was of prime concern to the two governments of Egypt and the Sudan, and to the committee appointed by UNESCO.

Some monuments, like Dakka and Kalabsha, were comparatively simple to dismantle; the rockcut tombs and chapels and the 'speos' temples posed a more difficult problem, especially in view of the poor state of preservation of some, and the friable nature of Nubian sandstone.

Each expedition was placed under an obligation to publish the results of its findings in as short a time as possible. In return for their co-operation in the scheme, the participating organizations were offered a fair share of the antiquities recovered. Important or unique objects were to be removed to the Cairo Museum of Antiquities, or, in the case of sites in Sudanese Nubia, to the Museum at Khartoum. In return for very great financial help, several small temples were offered as gifts to the other countries concerned, among them the temples of Dabod, Dendur and Tafa.

Now the campaign is over. It is probably true to say that never before has a large area been subjected to so intensive a study. The gain to history has been great, and in this book we have tried to show what that gain has been, or may in time be.

BUILDING THE HIGH DAM. The cutting of a diversion channel 200 feet deep is in progress; through this the Nile later flowed while the main dam was under construction.

CHAPTER I
Before History

At a time when Stone Age hunters roamed the desert and came to the river to drink, the Nile was much wider than it is at present. A number of surveys have been made in Egypt and Nubia to study the traces left by early man and their relationship with the geology of the region; as yet no complete picture has emerged and the prehistory of Nubia has yet to be written. Some facts, however, have been established. In the cliffs bordering the present Nile Valley there are a series of descending gravel terraces formed by the gradually shrinking river. Among the tell-tale signs found there are the shells of a small mollusc, the Nile oyster (*Cleopatra bulimoides*) which is still common in the Nile; their presence is an excellent indicator of the limit of the high Nile at a particular period. In the gravels of the lower terraces, rough stone axes of Palaeolithic man have been found a hundred feet above the present level. Some oscillations in the climate correspond with variations in the rate of fall, but it may generally be said that from 12,000 BC onwards there was progressive desiccation as the river shrank to its present size in historic times; at the gradually lowering water's edge, successive levels of human occupation have been found.

In the Sahara Desert, there are many signs that the northern part of Africa was once far more fertile, and enjoyed a considerable rainfall. Ancient watercourses can be traced in regions now completely arid, and the fossil remains of reptiles and aquatic mammals can be found. Perhaps as late as 5000 BC, prehistoric man hunted animals which have long since moved many hundreds of miles south into inner Africa. In the desert, and near the banks of the Nile, the hunters scratched or hammered on rock, or occasionally painted pictures of creatures which were, then, familiar sights: elephants and ostriches, giraffes, lions, oryx and antelope. Some of these animals may have

survived in the area but the elephants and giraffes must have left before recorded history. Many hundreds of these rock-drawings, or petroglyphs as they are called, have been found in Nubia, rarely more than a few hundred yards from the river, and often on the over-hanging ledges or rock shelters in which the artists made their homes. A survey, carried out between the two wars, of the area between the First and Second Cataracts recorded some hundreds of these drawings, but in the recent campaign teams of scientists have been engaged in a more thorough and far-reaching search and many more have been found and copied. It is not easy to date these pictures, though some of the later ones are clearly the work of the inhabitants of Nubia in historic times, even quite late in history.

Not only climatic change, but also the destructiveness of man must have chased some animals south. The hippopotamus was hunted in Pharaonic times; it is not now found north of Khartoum. Deforestation too must have played its part. We know that there were once plenty of trees in Nubia and that they were felled for boat-building (see p. 18). There were vineyards in Nubia, too, in the time of the New Kingdom and large herds of cattle were raised; perhaps overgrazing was another cause of the eventual dessication of the land.

Some time between 10,000 and 7,000 BC, Neolithic man learned two techniques vital for his future development: the cultivation of grain and the domestication of animals. The first agriculturalists are probably to be sought in the uplands of Western Asia, in Iran or Kurdistan. Whether the transition from a hunting economy to a pastoral or a farming one was made independently in Africa, or whether, as many think, these skills were transmitted to the Nile Valley through contact with the peoples of Mesopotamia or Syria is still an unsolved problem. Communities of fisherfolk living on the edge of the Nile near Khartoum as late as 4000 BC (if reliance can be placed on the dating of organic matter known as the Carbon 14 method) knew neither agriculture nor domestication. They were Negroes, and they manufactured brown pottery bowls decorated by combing with catfish bones in imitation of basketry – an indication that the earliest pots may have been baskets of reeds, daubed with clay to make them watertight. Their Neolithic successors made finer wares and wore necklaces of stone or of ostrich-shell; they were still primarily hunters and fishermen, but they had begun to domesticate the goat. Some of the artefacts of these people have close parallels in the early cultures of Egypt itself; recent surveys in Nubia may link the two. Very little is yet known about the prehistory of Nubia before about 3000 BC, though the results of the recent campaign should help to build a clearer picture.

It appears that though the deserts on either side were now arid, the Nile flood, by reason of heavy rainfall at the sources of the White Nile and the Blue Nile, was more copious, and the flood plain wider than it is today. The population was sparsely scattered in small village settlements, probably consisting of clusters of round, straw-thatched huts. They wore fringed leather kilts, cultivated small patches of wheat and barley, and herded cattle and goats. Their dead were wrapped in matting and buried in shallow graves together with red burnished pottery rimmed with black, flint knives and ivory ornaments. Ivory and ebony from the Sudan are found also in the graves of predynastic Egyptians and there must have been free communication along the Nile; the grave goods too are similar, though Nubian graves are as a rule much poorer than those of their northern neighbours. Measurement of skulls from the cemeteries in both countries shows that they were of similar racial type. It has even been suggested by some scholars that Lower Nubia was colonized by Egyptians during the predynastic period, either because of an increase in population leading to land-hunger in Upper Egypt, or as a result of political upheaval which may have caused refugees to flee beyond the border. In the absence of written history, this must remain conjecture.

CHAPTER II
The Door of the South

THE ROCK OF OFFERINGS AT ASWAN. The scene is imagined, as it might have been during the Old Kingdom, more than four thousand years ago. The leaders of a caravan, reaching the rock, pause to pour libations and offer prayers to the gods of the cataract region for a safe journey into the perilous unknown.

On the edge of the desert, high above the Nile, and visible from the town of Aswan, is a solitary mushroom-shaped rock perhaps ten feet high. A wide track leads up to it from the valley and, passing round it on the western side, stretches on and away out of sight over the rocky desert towards the south. Few now visit this place, but it is the starting-point of the Elephantine Road, one of the oldest roads in the world. Up to this rock the Egyptian caravan leaders of the Old Kingdom plodded with their donkey trains laden with waterskins and provisions, and as they passed the rock, they paused to pour

15

a small cupful of precious water as a libation, with a prayer to Khnum, the ram-headed god of the cataract region, to Satis the goddess who wore a head-dress of gazelle's horns, and to Anukis of the feathery crown; having made their petitions for a safe journey, they piled up a little cairn of stones near the rock and set the cup on it. Sometimes those who knew how to write paused long enough to scratch their names on the rock; these short inscriptions are still to be seen, and so are the cairns and broken potsherds. Many of the names are those of travellers to Nubia in the time of the Old Kingdom, some four thousands five hundred years ago.

It has been said that in the latter part of the prehistoric period, the civilization of Nubia differed very little from that of Upper Egypt. In Egypt, however, a little before 3000 BC remarkable advances began to be made. Men learned to perfect copper tools and to work more skilfully in stone, to build large monuments in mudbrick and stone and to fashion beautiful and intricate objects in many different materials. Most remarkable of all, they learned the art of writing. But Nubia now lagged behind, and the few simple grave-goods found there, in tombs contemporary with those of the early dynasties of Egypt, continue the traditions of the predynastic age. While the Egyptians were beginning to build themselves tombs of stone masonry, decorated and furnished with every luxury, the Nubians were still buried in a crouching position in shallow graves or rectangular pits, with a few pots and a flint knife or so, some beads and a stone palette for grinding eye paint, as their equipment for life in the hereafter. Only occasionally has a richer burial been found, containing objects of metal, stone and green-blue faience im-ported from Egypt; no doubt these were the tombs of chieftains. The people who made the pottery and other objects characteristic of this phase of civilization in Nubia are called by some archaeologists the A-Group, while the yet more impoverished phase contemporary with the Egyptian Old Kingdom used to be known as the B-Group; the latter term has however gone out of use, since there seems to be no evidence of a change of population; merely a decline in numbers due to causes which we shall now relate.

The Egyptians of the early dynastic period regarded the land immediately south of the First Cataract as a country to be plundered, by force of arms if necessary. The earliest evidence of their warlike intent is a crude carving incised on a rock on the west side of the Nile near Buhen, where the Second Cataract begins, some two hundred miles south of Aswan. It seems to repre-

16

sent a river encounter: a chieftain, whose hands are bound behind his back, is led prisoner by King Djer, whose name is clear to read though he is not himself depicted. Under a boat corpses float in the water, and another bound figure, labelled 'the Nubian', is pierced with arrows. Egyptian historical records tells us that about two hundred years later, another Egyptian ruler, Snofru, the father of Khufu, the Pharaoh who built the Great Pyramid and himself a mighty pyramid-builder, sent a campaign into Nubia in which 200,000 head of cattle were captured and 7,000 men and women carried off into slavery; the numbers may be exaggerated, but may not be greatly so. Between 1961 and 1963 a number of A-Group settlements were excavated by a Russian expedition sent by the Soviet Academy of Sciences, near the Wady Allaki in Lower Nubia. Most of the pots, in the opinion of the excavators, were connected with the production of milk and butter, and the area may well have been cattle-grazing country, subject to raiding by the Egyptians.

After about 2700 BC, if not before, Nubia was also exploited by the Egyptians for its mineral wealth. It is not known whether the copper mines sixteen miles south of Aswan were worked so early, but copper was certainly found much farther south, somewhere in the hills near the Second Cataract. One of the unexpected results of the Egypt Exploration Society's excavation of Buhen was the discovery of a sizable town of the Old Kingdom. The presence of copper slag, together with charcoal and gouts of pure copper from the crucibles, proved that the metal had been smelted there near the river's edge. Almost all the pottery was of Egyptian manufacture, and the clay impressions of seals from jars, bags and papyrus scrolls were further evidence that the colony had been supplied from Egypt and had maintained contact with the homeland by a courier service. The seals were those of a number of

the Fourth and Fifth Dynasty Egyptian kings: Khafra, the builder of the second pyramid, and his son Menkaure or Mycerinus among them. Another small colony must have been concerned with the quarrying and dispatch of diorite, a hard crystalline stone which was in demand for royal statues, vases and the like. The diorite quarries have been discovered far out in the western desert west of Abu Simbel, whence the heavy lumps were transported on donkey-back to the Nile bank, and then on rafts to the First Cataract. Here and there along the fifty-mile route to the river little dumps of the stone were found, as if some donkey had collapsed and his burden had been abandoned. In the Sixth Dynasty King Merenre had five channels cut in the First Cataract above Aswan, to facilitate the transport of barges bringing stone. The official in charge of the task describes how the chieftains of Irthet, of Wawat, of Yam, and of Madjoi assisted him by hewing acacia wood to make the barges; and drawings on granite boulders in the neighbourhood depict him receiving the homage of three of the four tribal sheikhs, the chieftain of Yam being absent from the scene. Wawat and Irthet were probably regions of Lower Nubia; the Madjoi were nomads, perhaps ancestors of the modern Beja. The land of Yam was further away; it may have been the region south of the Second Cataract.

As the courts of the Old Kingdom monarchs grew more luxury-loving and the demands for enrichment of the temples grew, expeditions were ever more frequently sent overland to the far south, to barter beads, knives and other trinkets for the exotic produce of the Sudan. The starting place of these expeditions, as we have already said, was Aswan just north of the First Cataract. The Greeks called Aswan Elephantine and its Egyptian name was Yebu, 'Ivory Town', for it was the place where the early tribes had brought their wares to market, trading the prized elephant tusks for whatever manufactured goods they needed. The Arabic name, As-Suân, means the market.

The residence of the nobles and the headquarters of the garrison were on an island in the river, now known as Elephantine Island. Here lived the nomarchs, princes who governed the most southerly nome, or administrative district, of Egypt. Their tombs can still be seen from the ruins of the town: looking north a row of squarely cut openings are apparent high up in the cliff on the west side of the Nile. The tombs have long since been rifled of their treasures, but the inscriptions on their walls preserve the identity and something of the life-story of their owners. These servants of Pharaoh bore titles such as 'Nomarch of Yebu, Keeper of the Door of the South, Caravan Leader who brings the produce of the foreign counties to his Lord'. From Yebu they set out on long journeys to the south to obtain tusks of ivory and logs of ebony, leopard skins, ostrich feathers, sacks of myrrh and precious stones. Their journeys occupied many months and they were in danger of attack from Nubian desert tribes. Their autobiographies, inscribed in hieroglyphics on the walls of their tombs, constitute the earliest chapter in the history of the exploration of Africa.

One of them, Sabni, whose titles include that of 'Royal Seal-bearer, Governor of the South and Sole Companion (of the King)', describes how two survivors had come to him with the news that his father had been killed while, as nomarch, he was leading an expedition to the Sudan, and how he set off at once with an armed escort, and 'one hundred asses with me, carrying ointment, honey, oil and linen . . . in order to make presents to people in those countries of the Nubians'. Sabni found his father's body and like a dutiful son, placed it in a coffin, presumably after a rough and ready attempt to preserve it, and brought it back to Egypt for proper burial. Ahead of the cortège he sent fast couriers bringing gifts for the King, including an elephant's tusk three cubits long (about four and a half feet); the messengers were to tell the King that a tusk double the size was on its way, and also that Sabni had managed to recover his father's body. A royal messenger brought the King's reply by boat, full of praise for the filial act, together with materials for the proper embalming of the body; 'then I buried this my father,' says Sabni, 'in his tomb in the necropolis; never before was one of his rank so splendidly buried.'

Another of the nobles of Elephantine, Harkhuf by name, led no less than four expeditions through Nubia to the Sudan, the first, as a young man, with his father. His journeys took seven or eight months and must have led him far south. On his third journey he discovered that the chieftain of the distant land of Yam had been called away to smite the Libyans of the western desert 'as far as the western corner of heaven' so he went after him and acted as a mediator between the two warring tribes; he then returned home to Egypt with 'three hundred donkey-loads of incense, ivory, *heknu* (whatever that may be), grain, panther skins, ivory or throwing sticks and every good product'; the grateful prince of Yam gave him an escort and safe-conduct through the intervening stretch where his caravan might be raided by desert tribes.

Harkhuf's last expedition was even more successful, for by a stroke of luck he managed to secure a treasure much desired in Egypt . . . a dwarf whom he brought back as a kind of human pet to caper for the King of Egypt and make him laugh. King Pepy, who was only a small boy at the time (he lived to be nearly a hundred, and can claim the longest reign in history), was delighted at the news and sent an enthusiastic letter to greet the returning caravan, a letter which Harkhuf was so proud to receive that he had it copied verbatim on the wall of his tomb. In it the King expressed his excitement and urged Harkhuf to take great care of the little man: 'When he embarks with thee in the boat, appoint trusty men to sit beside him on each side of the vessel; take care lest he fall into the water! When he sleeps at night, set trusty men to sleep at his side in the tent; inspect him ten times a night! My Majesty desires to see this pygmy more than all the gifts of Sinai and of Punt.' It was a long journey, but presumably the caravan reached Egypt safely: the letter ends with promises of a rich reward.

Nubian graves of the period of the later Old Kingdom are rarely found, and their contents are poor; even beads and ornaments are scarce in these burials, and the pottery is of inferior workmanship. Everything points to a decline both in culture and in population. The Egyptians must be held responsible. They raided cattle, and carried off men and women to slavery. From the poverty-stricken land, other Nubians migrated north of their own free will to take service in Egypt, or to serve in the Egyptian army in Asia.

These are the 'peaceful Nubians' mentioned in a decree of King Pepy I as living in the Memphis area around 2300 BC. Some of their memorial-stones have been found farther south, at Gebelein in Upper Egypt, where they adopted the Egyptian way of life and burial customs; some of them even have Egyptian names. In the reliefs carved on their grave stones they are distinguished from native Egyptians by their darker colour, their bushy hair bound with a fillet, and their distinctive dress, a sash and a sporran worn over the usual Egyptian-type short kilt. They sometimes had their hunting dogs carved on the stela, along with their wives and children, as if the dogs, too, were regarded as members of the family.

*STONE GATEWAY IN THE BYZANTINE FORTRESS OF TUMÂS. The excavation of
this site was undertaken by the Spanish National Committee for Nubia. (See Chapter VIII.)*

THE 'BELLY OF STONES'. Broken water and bush-covered islets in a reach of the Second Cataract, above Buhen.

CHAPTER III
The Frontier Fortified

Not long after the death of the old king, Pepy II, in about 2260 BC, Egypt, too, fell upon evil days. The kingdom was divided, several local rulers claiming sovereignty. Overseas trade was at an end, the vulnerable frontiers were over-run by desert raiders. During this unhappy interlude, which historians of Egypt call the First Intermediate Period, changes were taking place in Nubia. Into the depopulated valley of the Nile came immigrants who are known, for want of a more precise identity, as the C-Group People.

No one knows whence they came, but it is generally supposed that it was from the south. Recent geological and climatological studies have shown that there had been considerable progressive desiccation in the region up-stream of the Second Cataract during the third millennium, and a sharp and sudden decrease of rainfall at the beginning of the second, which turned the land of Kush, as it was now called, from a prairie into a desert. It may be that these arid conditions, and the consequent failure of their old grazing grounds, drove the cattle-raising C-Group People northwards in search of pasture for their herds. Most of their settlements are found at the mouths of dry ravines near the Nile, where silt had been deposited by the river; they were therefore not nomads, but pastoral agriculturalists. Fishing and hunting must have supplemented their diet. Bones of cattle, goats and sheep were found in their graves and the skulls of these animals were often set above the burials. Sometimes rough stone pillars set up to mark the graves had figures of cattle incised roughly on them. Some of the rock drawings near the river, depicting bulls or cows or small cattle, may be their work.

C-Group cemeteries have been found in Egypt as well as in Nubia: the most northerly is at Kubanieh, north of Kom Ombo. In Nubia their burial-places, at first shallow graves surrounded by a ring of stones, developed into tombs of more elaborate design with a stone-built subterranean chamber and a circular superstructure, sometimes with an adjoining chapel for which Egyptian influence may be responsible. The people themselves were not Negroes, though they were probably dark-skinned. They wore leather garments and ornaments carved from stone, bone or shell. Their pottery is handsome and distinctive: for the most part black bowls incised with patterns of stripes. Some of the graves also contained one or two objects of Egyptian manufacture.

Soon after 2000 B C a new dynasty came into power in Egypt. Some fifty years earlier, a Theban ruler called Mentuhotep had succeeded in reuniting the country and, during the course of a long reign, in restoring prosperity at home and to a certain extent, Egypt's prestige abroad. It was a long time, however, before all the turbulent elements in Egypt could be reconciled to the rule of Thebes, and it was not until a strong and capable vizier named Ammenemes (or Amenemhet) seized the throne, that the country was completely brought under control and Egypt's arms carried abroad. Under the capable rule of the strong Pharaohs of the Twelfth Dynasty, the capital was moved north to Lisht, near the Fayyum region, whence a strong central government could the more easily control the powerful local governors of the provinces of Egypt, and send out trading expeditions overseas to Palestine and the Lebanon for oil, resin and timber, down the Red Sea for incense, and southwards for ivory, ebony and the other precious commodities of Sudanese trade. But in order to obtain free passage for these goods, and also to guard the southern frontier against possible incursions, a new policy was adopted towards Nubia: that of incorporating it within the frontiers of Egypt.

An army moved in and occupied Lower Nubia, not without resistance. An inscription of Ammenemes I records his arrival at Korusko 'to overthrow Wawat', at this time the name for all Lower Nubia as far as the Second Cataract. Successive kings of the dynasty left triumphal inscriptions commemorating their successes in the south; Sesostris I in about 1950 B C penetrated as far as Buhen, near Wady Halfa, where his general set up a commemorative stone (stela) depicting Nubian captives from various tribes of the Second Cataract region, with Kush at their head. At strategic points along the valley, fortresses were built. They were garrisoned by Egyptian troops supplemented by local levies. A papyrus found many years ago lists fourteen of these forts; there were probably more. One stood on the east bank at Kubban, guarding the route to the gold mines in the Wady Allaki, for thenceforward Nubian gold was to be one of the prime reasons for Egypt's desire to hold the south. On the opposite bank, another fort stood sentinel over the river at Ikkur. No less than seven fortresses watched over the rocky, fifty-mile stretch of the Second Cataract known as the 'Belly of Stones'. It is clear

THE FORTRESS AND TEMPLE OF SEMNA EAST. A section of the mudbrick girdle wall still stands to a considerable height at the south-west corner of the fort. On the left, the stone temple built by Tuthmosis III and Hatshepsut in honour of Sesostris III can be seen.

from the emplacement of these strongholds, some on islands, some on rocky eminences, that the southern frontier was a point of great defensive importance.

At Semna, near the southern end of the Cataract, the Nile is confined by a barrier of granite, and plunges through a narrow gap of unfathomable depth. On rugged heights at either side of this barrier, two forts were built, only a thousand feet apart, so that sentries could easily signal from one to the other across the rushing water. A third fort, Uronarti stood on an island only some three miles downstream. Inside the double fortifications of these fortresses, massively built of mudbrick strengthened with baulks of timber, the houses of the garrisons were set in orderly rows divided by paved streets. A roofed-over stairway leading steeply down to the river's edge at Semna West enabled water to be drawn in time of siege without exposing the defenders to

25

the arrows of the enemy.

On the rocks below the eastern fort at Semna, a number of hieroglyphic inscriptions mark the height of the Nile at its fullest flood in a number of years during the reign of Sesostris III, the king who may have been responsible for the reconstruction of the whole defensive complex, and of his successor, the administrator Ammenemes III. To obtain advance knowledge of the rate of rise of the Nile flood was of great, even vital, importance to the Egyptians, for their eager expectation could quickly be turned to dread if the floodwater threatened to be unduly copious. In that case, hasty precautions had to be taken in Egypt: it was every man to the river bank, to strengthen the dykes and to keep watch for any weak spots which might give way and bring disaster.

The puzzling thing about these flood-level marks at Semna is that they are some twenty-five feet higher than any level recorded in the twentieth century A D. This is remarkable even allowing for possible fluctuations of the general level of the river throughout the centuries. One explanation, proposed long ago, has recently been revived tentatively by Professor Vercoutter who studied the problem when he was excavating at Semna: that the Twelfth Dynasty kings of Egypt might have built a dam across the narrow channel and that the lake created by this barrier could have enabled shipping to sail far upstream and made trade with Africa easier and safer. Professor Vercoutter thought he could even identify traces of the dam still remaining at Semna East. If he is right, as well as being a frontier post, Semna must have been a busy port, in which goods from the south were disembarked and sent on their way northwards by donkey caravan along the Elephantine Road to Aswan. The road along the left bank actually ran through the fort itself. Other theories attribute the very considerable fall in the Nile level since 1800 B C to scouring of the river-bed by stones churned by the rushing waters, or to the fact that the general maximum level of the Nile flood may still have been generally higher at that time than it is today.

However this may be, there is no doubt that the main purpose of the fortress system was defence. Careful excavation and survey of many of the forts has been undertaken; being of mudbrick, nothing could be done to preserve them and their walls are already submerged and have melted under the rising waters. One of the most remarkable and best-preserved was Buhen, nearly opposite Wady Halfa, where Professor W. B. Emery and his British

THE RAMPARTS OF BUHEN. A rock-cut ditch, and a double rampart with loopholes and buttresses, defended Buhen from the landward sides; on the east the Nile guarded the town.

team worked for several years for the Egypt Exploration Society. They laid bare a large section of the ramparts and were able to reconstruct the whole plan of the fortress. Here, too, there was a double line of defence: Egyptian soldiers manning the outer defences stood behind a mudbrick breastwork with towers at intervals; in both the towers and the parapet there were two rows of triple loopholes, so designed that each archer had a choice of six slits pointing in six different directions, and could thus command a complete field of fire against any attackers who might have succeeded in clambering across the steeply-walled ditch. In the unlikely event of these outer defences being overrun, the attackers were still faced with a higher bastioned wall towering above them from which soldiers manning the inner battlements could rain down missiles. The only entrances to the town were by a water-gate on the quayside which could easily be defended, and by a narrow gateway flanked by towers on the landward side, approached by a drawbridge over

27

BUHEN: THE WESTERN DEFENCES. A rounded buttress and the loopholes in the outer ramparts can be seen.

the moat, which could be drawn on rollers into the town in time of danger.

Similar fortifications have been found at Mirgissa, Kor and other strongholds in the cataract region. One of these was Iken, the main trading post to which Nubians brought their wares for barter. A boundary stone set up at Semna makes the function of Iken clear, for it reads: 'Southern boundary made in the eight year (of the reign of Sesostris III) to prevent any Nubian from passing it downstream, either overland or by boat, or any herds of the Nubians, apart from those Nubians who come to trade with Iken or on any good business which may be transacted with them.' A little ray of light is shed on the life of the garrisons by another Twelfth Dynasty document, a papyrus which, on study, proved to be extracts from dispatches sent from Semna to the commanders of other forts in the area. The letters report apparently trivial comings and goings of the Nubians in the area and show that a close control was kept on all traffic, and that even the movement of herdsmen and their flocks in the desert was watched.

The forts must have been provisioned largely by water. When Professor Vercoutter was excavating at Mirgissa in 1962 and 1963 he came upon a remarkable and unique structure: a thick layer of Nile silt six feet wide had been spread along the river bank for a distance of more than two miles, and embedded in the mud at eighteen-inch intervals were logs of wood laid crosswise. What had been found was an ancient slipway, on which boats could have been dragged over the most difficult section of the cataract at that time of year, from December to July, when the river was so low that progress by water became impossible. The long tracks left by the hulls of the boats or of the sledges on which they may have been hauled, were found by the excavators in the dried mud, together with the footprints of the last man who had walked along the slipway, some four thousand years ago. By this means the forts of the 'Belly of Stones' could have been provisioned by river whatever the time of year.

THE FORTRESS OF BUHEN as it must have appeared in 1900 BC; a masterpiece of Egyptian military architecture. The reconstruction is based on the actual remains discovered by the Egypt Exploration Society.

What was the danger which threatened the Egyptians in Nubia? Were they afraid of the C-Group people? Hardly, for they seem at this time to have been living peacefully in their settlements alongside the Egyptians and to have been influenced more and more, as time went on, by Egyptian civilization. Or was it a threat from farther south, from the Land of Kush where perhaps some tribe or tribes, fierce nomads from the Sudanese desert, menaced and eventually overran the garrisons of Pharaoh? It may be that the answer to this question will never now be known. One archaeological discovery, however, made many years ago at Kerma on the Dongola reach of the Nile, suggests the presence in Kush of a barbarous and warlike people.

Here, two hundred miles south of Semna, the Egyptians of the Twelfth Dynasty had dared to build a trading post. Two large mudbrick towers built in Egyptian fashion stood on what had once been an island. One of them was a fort and a factory for the manufacture, apparently, of beads and objects of pottery and brightly coloured glaze. The other, two miles away, was a funerary chapel; an inscription found in it by the archaeologist Reisner gives the name of the place as 'The Walls of Ammenemes', one of the three Pharaohs of that name having presumably been the founder of the establishment. Near the chapel were a number of graves. Some of those buried appeared to have been Egyptian officials who had lived and died, and perforce been buried, in this faraway place . . . a fate which was dreaded by all Egyptians. To them it was of vital importance to be buried in one's own country with the proper rites, and with sons to carry on the proper performance of funerary offerings. The bodies, it was noticed, were interred facing north, looking towards home, their sandals ready for the long journey their souls must take, and food and drink set ready beside them.

The largest mounds, however, contained burials of quite un-Egyptian type. Under a large tumulus, between two and three hundred people had been buried. In the central chamber a chieftain lay on a bed, and in the corridors around, the rest, probably his retainers, men, women and children, had been buried alive, presumably to keep him company and serve him in the next world. Here, then, was proof of the horrible and barbaric practice of human sacrifice in a settlement which had apparently been run by the Egyptians themselves! Reisner even deduced that the owners of the tombs had been Egyptian governors, for in one of the largest of the tumuli, the statue of an Egyptian noble was found, together with that of his wife. This official, whose tomb at Asyut in Middle Egypt was already well known to Egyptologists, must, Reisner concluded, have been a Governor in the Dongola region. He must have died at Kerma and been buried there rather than in the tomb prepared for him in Egypt, and the local people had insisted on according him at his funeral the quite un-Egyptian honour of wholesale human sacrifice; since there were a number of these burials, it was suggested, the practice must have continued for several generations. Nevertheless most Egyptologists found it hard to believe that Egyptians, to whom the idea was quite foreign and, at that period, abhorrent, would have countenanced such a practice. Moreover there were other objects in the graves, such as royal statuettes, and Old Kingdom vases, which could not be accounted for by this theory. What is more probable is that these were native Nubian chieftains, buried at some time after the Twelfth Dynasty, when the Egyptians had already left or been driven out of Kerma, and that they had acquired these things from the north at a time during the disorders of the Second Intermediate Period, when tombs in Egypt were being rifled and it was possible for such loot to come into the market.

In the reign of Sesostris III (1878–1843 BC) Egyptian activity in Nubia was intensified, perhaps as a result of some movement of tribes threatening the security of the land of Wawat. Sesostris first recut or cleared the artificial channels down which warships were drawn through the dangerous rapids of the First Cataract. One of these canals, we are told, was no less than two hundred and fifty feet long and thirty feet wide. In the eighth year of his reign, when all was ready, he marched south to 'smite the miserable Kush'. This expedition was followed by another; then a third and a fourth. In the third, undertaken in his sixteenth year, he ruthlessly plundered the enemy. 'I captured their women,' he says in a commemorative inscription, 'I reached their wells, I killed their cattle, I reaped their grain and set fire to their fields.' For centuries afterwards, Sesostris was worshipped as a god in the Second Cataract region; many of the fortresses were strengthened by him and he may have been the king who was responsible for the Semna defences. After his death, the dynasty lost impetus and ended obscurely.

In the troubled times that followed, called by historians the Second Intermediate Period, the Egyptians gradually lost control of Nubia. The fortresses were captured, looted and burnt and the fate of the garrisons may be imagined. Kush took her revenge. Meanwhile during this troubled period

31

foreigners had been pouring into the Delta of Egypt from the north-east, and eventually became so numerous that an Asiatic dynasty, later known as the Hyksos, seized the throne about 1730 BC and ruled Egypt for a time. These shepherd kings – 'Rulers of Foreign Lands', as the Egyptians called them – absorbed Egyptian culture and were patrons of art and learning, but they never won a place in the hearts of the people of Egypt and in later years the memory of them was hateful. Their rule lasted, according to one of the most reliable historical papyri, a hundred and ten years. When it ended, a new era began both for Egypt and for Nubia.

THE TEMPLE OF HATSHEPSUT AT SEMNA WEST. The small temple dedicated to a Nubian god, Dedwen, stood on a craggy height overlooking the turbulent Nile. (See p. 35.)

CHAPTER IV
The Gold of Kush

'We are in possession of our Egypt; Elephantine is strong, and the Middle Land is with us as far as Cusae.' So, complacently, spoke the advisers of King Kamose in Thebes, the capital of Upper Egypt, counselling a policy of non-interference with the Hyksos who ruled the north of Egypt from their capital Avaris in the eastern Delta. But Kamose, scorning their cowardice, answered them angrily, 'What use, pray, is this strength of mine, when one foreigner is in Avaris and another in Kush, and I sit cheek by jowl with an Asiatic and a Nubian, each in possession of his part of Egypt's territory, and I cannot even reach Memphis?' The large number of seals bearing the names of Hyksos kings found at Kerma suggests that this town was the headquarters or capital of the native rulers of Kush at this time, and that the great tumuli we have already described were their burial-places. According to Kamose the Hyksos king, Apophis, was in alliance with the ruler of Kush, but a messenger bearing proposals for a joint attack on the Thebans, fortunately for Egypt, fell into Kamose's hands and the plot was foiled.

The war of liberation was carried to a successful conclusion under his leadership, though he did not live to see the final triumph. The Hyksos were driven from their beleaguered capital and chased into Palestine. His brother Ahmose, who succeeded him, led the victorious army in pursuit; he then turned to deal with Kush. Once again much of Nubia was quickly reduced and the area of the Second Cataract occupied; a small temple of Ahmose at Buhen is the earliest evidence of the resettlement of the district by Egyptian occupation troops.

Patriotic fervour and the excitement of plunder now inspired the Egyptians with a warlike spirit unprecedented in their history. New weapons developed in the north by newcomers in Syria and Mespotamia, were now in their hands: the powerful composite bow, the light war-chariot drawn by horses, the slashing sword and the use of toughened bronze. King's sons were taught to ride and shoot and to lead their armies in battle; they prided themselves on their physical strength and boasted of being able to outdo their soldiers in displays of archery. Ahmose's successors led their armies north and south,

33

and by 1520 had penetrated Syria and reached the Euphrates.

In the south their ambitions turned towards Kush itself, the country below the Second Cataract. Here the valley was wider than in Upper Nubia and the soil more fertile, there was grazing for cattle, and a considerable agricultural population living in villages. Control of this region, now known as the Dongola reach, meant direct access to the caravan routes by which exotic southern products, once brought by the nomarchs of Elephantine, could again be obtained; it was, moreover, necessary to ensure that there was no danger of another tribal coalition threatening the security of Egypt as the Ruler of Kush had done in Kamose's time. A third incentive was the need for manpower; when the first flush of triumph was over, enthusiasm for campaigning abroad began to wane, but more and more soldiers were needed, and Kushite levies began to be trained to strengthen the thin ranks of Egypt's forces abroad. The Medjay or Madjoi tribe, in particular, were in demand for army service in Egypt itself, where they served as a kind of police force to keep order and patrol the desert.

The early kings of the Eighteenth Dynasty, beginning with Ahmose himself, took great pains with the conquest and settlement of Kush. The frontier was moved south, first to Tombos beyond the Third Cataract, which was fortified – an inscription there is dated to the reign of Tuthmosis I – and then farther upstream along a navigable stretch of the Nile to Karoy, the region of Napata near the Fourth Cataract. Karoy (the name is preserved in the modern Kareima) is stated by Tuthmosis III to be the limit of his jurisdiction. The town grew up in the shadow of a remarkable flat-topped hill, a kind of small Table Mountain, called today the Gebel Barkal; the Egyptians regarded it as a holy mountain, the abode of the Lord of the Winds, and at its foot a temple was built in honour of the local god, whom the Egyptians identified with Amun, their own national deity. Tuthmosis III boasted that his frontiers stretched 'from the marshes of Asia to the Horns of the Earth', perhaps another designation of the hilly Barkal region though there are traces of Egyptian enterprise farther upstream at Kurgus, where the overland route from Korusko joins the Nile, and even perhaps at Meroe above the Atbara junction, where a few Egyptian objects of Eighteenth Dynasty date have been found.

As soon as news came of the death of Tuthmosis I, the tribes of Lower Nubia broke into rebellion. The new pharaoh, Tuthmosis II, sent an army and the revolt was ruthlessly crushed: 'The army of His Majesty overthrew these barbarians. By command of His Majesty not one of their males (i.e. the men of the chieftains' families) was left alive, except one of the children of the miserable ruler of Kush who was captured alive and brought as a prisoner with their people to the place whither His Majesty had commanded them, and set under the feet of the Good God (the Pharaoh). His Majesty made an appearance upon his throne of audience and the living prisoners were brought before him, whom his army had captured. This land was made subject to His Majesty as it had been formerly, and the people rejoiced, the chiefs were joyful, they gave praise to the Lord of the Two Lands. . . .' Whatever the real feelings of the Nubians may have been, the action taken was effective and, for a long time, no further revolts took place.

Tuthmosis II was followed by his sister-wife Hatshepsut, one of the most remarkable figures in Egyptian history. Set in charge of her young nephew (another Tuthmosis), the rightful heir to the throne, as regent she soon seized the throne for herself and ruled Egypt for the next twenty-two years. Though she adopted the insignia of a king and is depicted in male attire in her temples, she could not – or perhaps would not – lead armies into battle, and her reign (1503–1482 BC) was peaceful, a period of commercial expansion and considerable building activity. The graceful little temple at Buhen with its fluted columns was built by her orders, and so were the small temples at Faras, Semna East and Semna West. These stone buildings replaced earlier, Twelfth Dynasty brick temples, traces of which were revealed when the New Kingdom ones had been removed for re-erection elsewhere during the recent campaign.

No sooner was Hatshepsut dead than her nephew, Tuthmosis III, long grown to manhood and chafing at restraint, bitterly gave orders that her memory be erased from the record. Wherever her name appeared, it was to be obliterated. The temples at Buhen and Semna, and a shrine at Ibrim, bear his name, but on close examination of some of the cartouches (as the royal names in their oval frames are called) it can be seen that the name Hatshepsut has been rubbed down, and the stone surface recut. Almost at once, the King set out to achieve his ambition to conquer an empire in Asia. In seventeen strenuous campaigns he brought Palestine and the Lebanon under Egyptian control and reached his father's boundary stone at the Euphrates river near Carchemish. The conquered territory was garrisoned and set under military control, and tribute flowed into the coffers of the administration.

At the same time a greater effort was now made to incorporate the land of Kush within the boundaries of Egypt. The country had already been settled by colonies of Egyptians, and the Nubians became Egyptianized by contact with them. Nubian princes were taken to be educated in Egypt, and returned to bring civilization to their people. At this time Nubia began to achieve some measure of prosperity. In view of the distance from the capital, the Pharaohs found it advisable to put a viceroy in charge of the whole country south of the First Cataract. He was known as 'The Prince (King's Son), Overseer of the Southland', the former title indicating not royal birth but rather a designation of rank, like the more recent 'Pasha'. He was further dignified by the title of 'Fanbearer on the King's Right Hand' and is generally referred to as the Prince of Kush. Both Kush, the southern region, and Lower Nubia or Wawat, were under his jurisdiction. Each of the two provinces was under a deputy who was responsible to the viceroy.

The Prince of Kush lived in viceregal splendour, with a large staff. His duty was to administer Nubia efficiently, keep order and ensure the safe passage of caravans, and forward the annual tribute of his province. The names of most of the viceroys are known; their inscriptions and their images are found on rocks and in temples everywhere. Recent archaeological exploration has discovered one or two new ones; at Arminna West, for instance, the expedition led by Professor Kelly Simpson found inscriptions which mention three, all of whom were probably in office at the very beginning of the Eighteenth Dynasty and therefore earlier than the first hitherto known. Several names of viceroys have been effaced from the stones on which they were carved, indicating perhaps that in times of political unrest, or for some personal reason, they fell from power.

One of the most important responsibilities of the viceroys was to see to it that Nubia produced its quota of gold every year. As it had been in the time of the Middle Kingdom if not earlier, gold was the principal export from Nubia. It was needed in Egypt to provide a suitably magnificent environment for the court, to reward faithful servants of the Crown and to fulfil the insatiable demands of the gods for the equipment of their temples. Secondly, gold was a valuable export. The second millennium was an age of international diplomacy in which a number of almost equal powers were in competition one with another; every king in western Asia vied with his rivals in the splendour of his court and all competed in the desire to obtain that most splendid adornment of all, the glittering and untarnishable gold. And most of it came from Nubia. By a fortunate chance, some of the letters written by these monarchs to the Egyptian kings Amenophis III and Amenophis IV have been preserved, and in most of these the request for gold is reiterated to the point of tedium. 'In my brother's land,' writes the King of Mitanni, 'gold is as common as dust; send me therefore much gold!' and similar demands are made by the kings of Assyria and Babylonia. This put Egypt in a very strong position, both politically and economically, for the other powers were anxious not to offend her, and in return for the gold they sent presents of all sorts, horses and chariots, precious stones and all kinds of manufactured articles, and the value of these commodities was carefully reckoned in terms of the weight and quality of the gold sent. Western Asia, in fact, was 'on the gold standard'.

Nubian gold was mined in the eastern desert; 'gold of Wawat' came for the most part from the Wady Allaki area, and 'gold of Kush' from mines in the mountains farther south. 'Gold of the water' was no doubt alluvial gold obtained by panning. By the side of the Nile at Faras and other places in Nubia there are shallow, rectangular basins cut in the rock, known locally as *hammams* (baths); these were almost certainly installations for washing gold, and not wine-presses as used to be thought.

The rock tomb in Egyptian Thebes of one of the viceroys of Kush, Huy by name, who held office in the reign of Tutankhamun, is decorated in the manner of all important nobles' tombs, with a series of paintings. One depicts the splendid ceremony at which the viceroy, coming in person to the capital, formally presents to the Pharaoh the annual tribute of his province. The native chieftains of Nubia, too, have come to do homage. They are of negroid appearance, with black or dark brown skins and their dress is barbaric and splendid: a leopard-skin cloak over one shoulder, a red embroidered sash, large earrings and an ostrich feather stuck in their bushy hair. One of them labelled 'Heqa-nefer, ruler of Mi'am' throws himself on the ground in obeisance. 'The children of chieftains of every land' follow, the young men carrying trays of gold. Six princesses come with them; these are richly dressed in the Egyptian court fashion of the age, but their dark skins show that they are Nubians. The last of them, perhaps the youngest, rides in a chariot drawn by oxen – a novelty in Egypt – and is protected from the heat

NUBIAN GRANDEES BRING TRIBUTE TO PHARAOH IN THE TRAIN OF THEIR VICEROY. From the Tomb of Huy, Viceroy of Nubia in the reign of King Tutankhamun.

of the sun by ostrich-feather fans.

In front of the chieftains, on the ground, gold is heaped; gold in rings, gold in lumps, bags of gold-dust and elaborate set-pieces of intricate craftsmanship depicting the land of Nubia and its produce. As well as gold there are heaps of elephant tusks, logs of ebony, lumps of carnelian and other stones, leopard skins, furniture of several kinds, bows and arrows and decorated shields, cattle with ornaments on their horns, giraffes' tails to be used as fly-whisks, and even a live giraffe.

Of Heqa-nefer we now know a little more, for in excavating on the east bank of the Nile at Toshka in 1961 Professor Kelly Simpson found the rock-cut tomb of a ruler of Mi'am who is almost certainly to be identified with him. The inscriptions in his tomb tell us that he was brought up as a child in the royal harem in Egypt and educated with the royal princes; he was the proud bearer of titles which were habitually bestowed upon high-ranking dignitaries: 'Sandal-maker of the King', and 'Bearer of the Folding Chair of the Lord of the Two Lands'. One of his responsibilities was the regulation of river transport, and it may be in this capacity that he plays a leading role in the tomb of Huy. Nothing in Heqa-nefer's tomb betrays the fact that he was not Egyptian-born; had we not his likeness in his master's tomb at Thebes, we should never have guessed it. Another local chieftain, whose

38

decorated tomb was found at Debeira, bore the equally Egyptian name of Tehuty-Hotep. He was prince of Tehkhet, which is the modern Serra. On the walls of his tomb there are painted scenes showing him hunting in the desert on his chariot, seated among the trees in his garden, and banqueting with his wife to the accompaniment of an orchestra of musicians, all in the manner of a wealthy Egyptian nobleman; nothing but the names of his parents betrays the fact that he was a native of Nubia. Although the houses of such Egyptianized Nubian princes have not been found, it must be imagined that they would have been very much like houses of the upper class in Egypt at the time; no doubt many Nubians were persons of considerable wealth and status, provided that they co-operated with the viceroy and aided his administration.

Mi'am is the Aniba district, and in the desert near the modern town of Aniba a considerable town of the New Kingdom has been found, where commerce had flourished. Here and at Faras, Buhen and other town sites throughout Nubia there is evidence of gradually increasing Egyptian influence; in the cemeteries there is an admixture of Egyptian pottery, beads, amulets, mirrors and the like, with the Nubian pots and grave goods.

A mile or so upstream from Aniba, and on the opposite bank of the Nile, a huge rock towers above the river. The beetling cliffs are crowned by fortification walls, perhaps the work of the Meroites who made it a fortress. But recent excavations undertaken by the Egypt Exploration Society of London, under the direction of Professor Plumley, have found on the hill-top pieces of stone from buildings of Eighteenth Dynasty date, and an obelisk of Queen Hatshepsut, probably from a temple which once stood here. The place was sacred to Horus of Mi'am, the hawk-god whose modern incarnations still wheel above Nubian villages. At the base of the rock, and now submerged, are a series of shrines or chapels cut in the rock, carved and inscribed by officials of the New Kingdom in honour of the gods of Mi'am and the gods of the reigning pharaoh. The rising waters have by now turned the rock of Qasr Ibrim (Primis or Premnis, as it was called in classical times) into an island, but there is still time for one more season of excavation and it is hoped that this, the last of the Nubian sites to remain accessible, may yet yield a little more information about those who first fortified it.

A number of small temples commemorate the Pharaohs of the latter part of the dynasty in Nubia. They were located near large centres of population

ROCK-CUT TOMBS AT TOSHKA. *The open doorways belong to tombs of two local princes of Toshka, whose names are lost. That of Heqa-nefer, 'Royal Sandal-maker, Child of the Royal Nursery, Bearer of the folding chair of the Lord of the Two Lands, chief of oarsmen', is round the corner beyond the right-hand doorway.*

and were probably centres of worship for the native population as well as for Egyptian garrison troops. In many of them, the local gods of the district were worshipped alongside the deities of the Egyptian pantheon. Tuthmosis III built at Kalabsha and also erected the handsome little temple (to which his two successors added a forehall) at Amada. Traces of paint still remain on the reliefs, which are of the best New Kingdom style. The same can be said of the temples of Buhen and Semna, already mentioned. In 1963 and 1964 these two were dismantled, stone by stone, under the direction of a German engineer; each block and each column-drum was carefully protected from damage by wrappings; they were then transported by barge and lorry to Wady Halfa, whence they travelled by rail to Khartoum. They have now been re-erected in the garden of the museum. The temple of Amada, being compact and in good condition, could be moved bodily: at the expense of the French government it was mounted on wheels and moved backwards and uphill a mile or so on rails to the new site on which it now stands.

In the reign of Tuthmosis IV, and again in that of his son, Amenophis III, revolts broke out in Kush; perhaps the cause was unrest among the nomadic peoples west of the Nile Valley. Both necessitated strong military action, and in each case the Madjoi and other named tribes were brought to heel. It was Amenophis who erected one of the finest of all Nubian temples, the temple of Sulb or Soleb near the Third Cataract. Two of the magnificent couchant lions from this temple now lie at their ease, paw over resting paw, in the sculpture gallery of the British Museum. This same king, Amenophis, built in nearby Sedeinga a small temple for his consort, Queen Tiy. His long reign, from 1418 to 1380 BC, was a time when the prosperity of Egypt reached its highest peak. Tribute poured in from Africa and Asia, and trade with principalities from the Mediterranean to the Tigris Valley brought huge wealth to the royal coffers and to the temples which were the ultimate repositories of that wealth.

His son, the 'heretic king' Akhenaton, was a ruler of a different calibre. Alienating the orthodox priesthoods, and deserting his capital, he retired to a new city, Tell el Amarna, to devote himself to the new cult of the sun's disc, the Aton, which he had promoted. The consequences for the Egyptian empire in Asia were serious: armies were no longer despatched to trouble spots, and Egypt's dependencies began to throw off their allegiance. But Kush seems to have given no trouble, and the fact that Huy, in the time of Tutankhamun, only a few years after Akhenaton's death, could still command the homage of the Nubian chieftains (see p. 37) is an indication that in the south, all was well with the empire. A temple was built to the Aton at Kawa, opposite Dongola. The last king of the Eighteenth Dynasty, Horemheb, before his accession went as an army officer on a tour of inspection in Kush, and may again have visited it when, after the return to orthodoxy in Egypt, he became Pharaoh, for he is shown in one of his temples returning with Nubian prisoners.

This was a prosperous age for Nubia. Farmers worked the land as tenants of the royal estates, of the local princes or of the temples. The introduction of the shaduf, or bucket-lift, which first makes its appearance in the New Kingdom, probably greatly increased the area of arable land, with a conse-

THE TEMPLE OF AMADA. Built by Amenophis II about 1440 BC and embellished by his successors, this small temple contains some of the finest relief decoration in Nubia. It has now been removed and rebuilt some distance away on higher ground. (See also p. 85.)

quent increase in the population. Agriculture played a larger part in the life of the people than ever before; there is evidence of bee-keeping, the growing of date-palms and the cultivation of vineyards. Wells were dug in waterless areas where mining operations were in progress. Boatbuilding was an important industry and boats plied up and down the Nile carrying local produce from market to market. By contrast with the savage exploitation of the Old Kingdom Pharaohs, Egypt's rule appears now, in some sense, to have brought benefit to Nubia.

CHAPTER V
A God Among the Gods

Shortly before 1300 BC a vigorous family from the Delta of Egypt took over the reins of government. The first, a soldier named Ramesses who had been vizier and boon companion of the elderly king Horemheb, the last sovereign of the Eighteenth Dynasty, was already himself an old man when he came to the throne and reigned for only two years, but his son and grandson inherited his military gifts and, in a series of vigorous campaigns, made repeated bids to restore the old prestige of Egypt in Asia that had been all but lost in the years of inaction at Tell el Amarna and of quarrelling thereafter. Booty from Palestine and Syria again filled the state treasuries, and enriched the temples of the gods; new mines were opened and new routes explored and the gold of Kush once more flowed into the royal coffers.

The grandson, Ramesses II, was a remarkable figure, in some ways the most remarkable in Egyptian history. Not as successful in the field as his father Sety had been, he was anxious to appear so, and on the walls of the many splendid temples which he built, he commemorated in sculptures of heroic size, and in bombastic verse, the battle he had fought early in his reign against an army of Hittites and their allies at Qadesh in Syria, on the River Orontes. In fact, this encounter had very nearly ended in disaster, for the vanguard of the Egyptian army, advancing too rapidly, had marched into an ambush. The young king, by his personal bravery and a large slice of luck, had managed to extricate himself and his forces from the trap and to turn the tables on the enemy, driving the attackers back into the river. In five different temples the galloping chariots of the enemy are depicted, the King's heroic onset at the head of his troops, and the ensuing slaughter in which not one Egyptian is shown wounded or dying, but the enemy are everywhere overcome or in flight. Episodes in the combat are shown, sometimes more than once in different temples. A favourite scene was that of the discomfiture of the King of Aleppo, the son and viceroy of the Hittite king himself, who is shown being held upside down on the river bank by his own troops, half drowned and dripping, to make him disgorge the water he has swallowed in his ducking. Other Hittite grandees are being helped out of the water by their comrades.

43

THE GATE OF THE TEMPLE AT BEIT AL WÂLI. Like many others in Egypt and Nubia, this little temple was converted into a church by the early Christians. Note the slots of quarrymen's chisels on the block of stone in the foreground; by driving in wedges, the stone could be split.

Ramesses II reigned for no less than sixty-seven years (1304–1237 BC). Soon after the battle of Qadesh, hostilities came to an end and eight years later a treaty was signed with the Hittites. Thenceforward his long reign was devoted to building and to developing the country's resources. There was hardly a town in Egypt in which he did not build or enlarge a temple, and hardly a monument on which he did not leave his name carved bold and large. In Nubia no less than seven temples were built by him. One, the King's Temple at Abu Simbel, is the greatest of the monuments of Nubia, and one of the most impressive of all Egyptian temples. Almost all the Nubian temples of this date are of a similar plan: ascending from the river in a series of terraces with colonnaded courts. The inner pillared halls and sanctuary were of speos type, that is to say, cut deep into the rock. The approach was usually up a staircase flanked by hawk or ram-headed sphinxes, and the courts were divided by tower-like gateways known as pylons. In the lofty, dim interior of two of them, Abu Simbel and Gerf Husein, the central aisle is flanked by colossal figures of the King in the guise of Osiris, the mummified god of the dead. Figures of the King sitting in the company of the great gods

44

are carved in the round in the deepest sanctuary.

The little temple of Beit al Wali is probably the earliest of his monuments in Nubia. In its forecourt are lively scenes from the King's campaigns: on the north wall, he is depicted storming a Syrian fortress, while the vanquished enemy exclaims, 'Verily, there is none other like Baal, but this Ruler is his true son for ever!' On the southern wall incidents from a campaign in Nubia are shown; the King in his chariot charges into a crowd of Negroes, who flee in confusion towards their village. In the village a wounded man is being assisted by two comrades and a woman sits cooking under a palm tree, seemingly unconcerned at the approaching turmoil. A procession of Nubians bringing their tribute is also depicted; among the display of gold, skins, ostrich feathers and other treasures they bring a live panther, a lion, a giraffe, antelopes and an ostrich. A Negress in the procession is carrying two babies in a basket on her back and a little girl has a monkey on her shoulder. Such small details afford precious glimpses of life in Nubia in the thirteenth century BC.

WADY ES SEBU'A: THE PYLON OF THE TEMPLE. One of a pair of colossal figures of Ramesses II, who built the temple, can be seen at the gateway. The cornice which surmounts the sloping wall of the pylon is a characteristic feature of Egyptian architecture.

THE HYPOSTYLE HALL OF ABU SIMBEL, looking towards the sanctuary. Colossal figures of the king, pictured as Osiris god of the dead, stand four on either side against the pillars. They are about 35 feet in height.

Not less in interest, and far greater in size and sheer impressiveness, is the temple of Abu Simbel. There are, in fact, two temples, one hewn in a cliff set diagonally against the flow of the Nile and the other a little farther on, confronting the river squarely. The remarkable preservation of these temples is due to the perpetual wind of the high desert which, blowing down a gully between them, covered them deep in drift sand. It was not until 1812 that a Swiss traveller, Burckhardt, for the first time since antiquity, caught a glimpse of the great heads of the colossi and surmised that 'could the sand be cleared away, a vast temple might be discovered'. Giovanni Belzoni was to prove him right when, five years later, he and three companions dug away

INSIDE THE TEMPLE OF GERF HUSEIN. The remarkable figures on either side, 28 feet high, represent King Ramesses II in the guise of Osiris, the god of the underworld. Though smaller than their counterparts in the great hall at Abu Simbel, in the dim light they inspire feelings of awe.

46

the dune until, squeezing through the doorway and sliding down the sand inside, they found themselves in a vast rock-cut hall. The great temple, several times freed from sand, has rightly been counted among the most remarkable monuments left by the sculptors of antiquity. Not all critics agree as to its merit as a work of art, but none can deny its impressive grandeur. It is the supreme expression in stone of the concept of divine majesty and regal power, of which Ramesses II was himself the personification. In it, as in other temples which he built, Ramesses was depicted not only as a worshipper of the gods, but also as a god himself in their company. This led to the result, bizarre to our way of thinking but no doubt acceptable to an ancient Egyptian, that the Pharaoh is shown as a king in adoration of himself as a god. Four colossal statues of the King sixty feet high sit two on either side of the entrance; they should be visited by moonlight, when their huge, silent presence invokes a feeling of tremendous awe. In the sunlight they impress in a different way. They must have struck terror into the hearts of the simple superstitious Nubians who passed in their boats and sometimes brought propitiatory gifts. The value of Abu Simbel as propaganda for the might of Pharaoh was certainly not overlooked by its builder.

The temple faced east, and was dedicated to the god Rê-Harmachis, the rising sun. It was carefully orientated so that twice a year, for a few days in February and in October, the rays of the rising sun fell directly along the axis of the temple. No one who has been fortunate enough to be at Abu Simbel early on one of those special mornings can easily forget the hushed wait in the half-light of dawn, beneath the looming figures of the four colossi. As the rising sun appears above the eastern hills a golden glow spreads gradually downwards over the warm sandstone of the façade, and then the rays strike deep into the heart of the temple through the open portal, gilding the sentinel standing figures of the Osiris-king on either side of the main hall, and the lintels of each successive inner doorway in turn. At length they illuminate with soft light the four silent seated figures in the sanctuary, nearly two hundred feet inside the rock. It is good to know that in re-erecting the temple, care has been taken to preserve the exact orientation so that Rê-Harmachis once more rises above the purple hills to take possession of his shrine.

On the great north wall of the hypostyle hall (the great pillared entrance hall), Ramesses caused his artists to carve incidents from his day of triumph

48

FAÇADE OF THE GREAT TEMPLE OF ABU SIMBEL. The task of making a complete facsimile record of the reliefs and inscriptions in the temples has begun. Moored to the bank is the houseboat 'Hathor' used by the Egyptian Documentation Centre. The ancient mudbrick wall was built to contain drift sand which continually threatened to engulf the temple.

at Qadesh. The march of the Egyptian army towards the town is depicted, the setting-up of the camp, the flogging of the spies to extract information from them, and the clash of the two forces in their chariots. A critical moment in the battle is shown, when the King, surrounded by enemy chariots, is seeking to break through their lines. The city of Qadesh appears with the River Orontes flowing round it; the garrison within is watching the battle. Finally there is the rout of the enemy, the parade of prisoners before the god, and the counting of the grisly trophies of the slain.

The smaller temple at Abu Simbel is very different. It was built by the King in honour of his Queen, Nefertari, and was fittingly dedicated to a goddess, Hathor, Queen of Heaven, the patroness of women. Six standing colossi compose the façade; they represent, alternately, the King and the

49

THE TEMPLES OF ABU SIMBEL. Four colossal figures of King Ramesses II sit in front of the Great temple he excavated in the rock. The head of one has fallen and lies at its feet. The smaller temple, or Queen's temple, is seen on the right of the tree. A river of sand, blown by the wind down a rocky ravine, divides the two temples.

Queen, and smaller figures at their side are their children, daughters with the Queen and sons with the King. The large statues are thirty-five feet high, the children a mere ten. Within, the reliefs that decorate wall and pillars are graceful and somewhat feminine. Miss Amelia Edwards, whose account of Abu Simbel is as delightful as everything else that she wrote about Egypt, says this of it:

'On every pillar, in every act of worship pictured on the walls, even in the sanctuary, we find the names of Ramesses and Nefertari "coupled and inseparable". In this double dedication and in the unwonted tenderness of the style one seems to detect the traces of some event, perhaps of some anniversary, the particulars of which are lost for ever. It may have been a meeting; it may have been a parting; it may have been a prayer answered or a

wish fulfilled. We see, at all events, that Ramesses and Nefertari desired to leave behind them an imperishable record of the affection which united them on earth and which they hoped would reunite them in Amenti.* What more do we need to know?'

The problem of the salvage of the temples of Abu Simbel was one of the major topics of discussion among those responsible for the rescue of the monuments of Nubia, and it has had the lion's share of publicity in the press. Whatever method was decided upon, it was obviously going to cost an enormous sum of money, and contributions for this purpose were invited from the beginning. Large sums were initially given, and more, it was hoped, would be contributed before the work was completed. The method to be employed was the subject of long and often somewhat heated controversy. Many solutions were proposed. One entailed enclosing both temples in a huge encircling dam two hundred feet high, within which, at a lower level

* The underworld.

INSIDE THE QUEEN'S TEMPLE, ABU SIMBEL. Carved on the pillars are symbols of Hathor, the Queen's especial patron and goddess of love, to whom the temple was dedicated. Figures of the king and queen in the presence of gods and goddesses adorn the walls.

than the water outside, they could be viewed in their original setting; the visitor would arrive by boat, land on the edge of the dam, and descend by steps or by lift to a public garden which, it was envisaged, could add a modern touch to the scene. Another suggestion was to encase the temples in huge transparent domes, through which they could be viewed under water. Yet a third, and one which for a time found most favour, was the boldest and, at first sight, the most wildly improbable: an enterprising firm of Italian engineers offered to cut both temples free of the rock and raise them bodily, centimetre by centimetre, to the necessary height by means of hydraulic jacks. The weight, estimated in the case of the Great Temple as three hundred thousand tons, was far larger than any mass which had ever been lifted by this method before. Nevertheless the plan was pronounced by experts to be perfectly feasible. The cost of all these schemes, however, would have been enormous, and all but the last would have the disadvantage that seepage through the porous rock would entail the added expense of constant pumping, and perhaps endanger the fabric of the temples.

The final decision was at length taken: to cut up the temples into blocks and lift them piecemeal by crane, reassembling them on a higher level in suitable surroundings, and building up the landscape around them to some semblance of the original riverside setting. This is the same technique that has been used, on a smaller scale, for rock-cut temples and tombs in various parts of Nubia.

The cost of the work was estimated at eleven million pounds sterling ($26,400,000), of which the United Arab Republic has contributed one-third. The work, begun in 1963, was devised by Swedes and carried out by German contractors with Egyptian labour. First an arc-shaped coffer dam

ABU SIMBEL: FAÇADE OF THE QUEEN'S TEMPLE. On either side of the doorway, figures of King Ramesses alternate with those of his consort, Nefertari-beloved-of-Mut. An inscription, boldly and deeply incised in the rock, proclaims the king's titles and declares that His Majesty 'commanded a temple to be made in the hill as a work of eternity . . . nothing like it has ever been made before'.

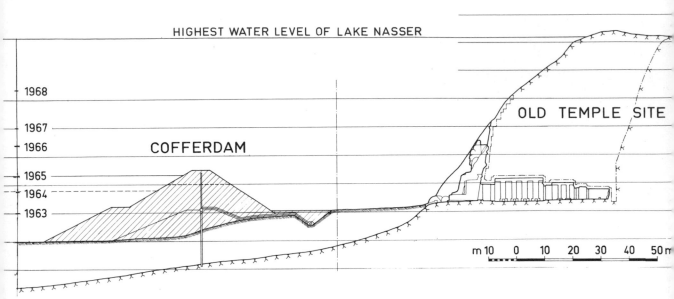

HIGHEST WATER LEVEL OF LAKE NASSER

1968

1967

1966   COFFERDAM   OLD TEMPLE SITE

1965

1964

1963

m 10   0   10   20   30   40   50 m

was built to protect the work from the already rising flood. Huge mounds of sand were then poured over the façades to protect the sculptures, and metal-lined tunnels were driven through to facilitate access to the interior and enable the cutting out to be accomplished in safety. In the fierce heat of summer, water had to be sprayed over the stone during the day, and at night the men worked by floodlight. Three hundred workers were employed. They lived in their own village and had their own hospital. One thousand nine hundred and thirty blocks or chunks of stone have been moved; they have been raised two hundred feet and re-erected 230 yards from the Nile. Re-construction began in March 1966.

Eighteen months later, the rebuilding finished, the construction of two large steel domes began. These served as background structures for land-scaping the temples, and will protect them from the eroding winds that constantly scour the desert on the cliff top. When this extraordinary task is finished, and the landscaping completed, the great seated figures of Ramesses will again gaze out over the Nile, assured, if not of immortality, at any rate of some hundreds more years of existence.

In 1236 BC, at the age of ninety or thereabouts, Ramesses the Great died

54

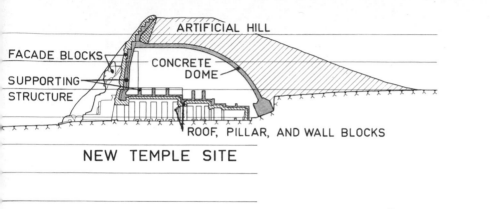

ARTIFICIAL HILL

FACADE BLOCKS

CONCRETE
DOME

SUPPORTING
STRUCTURE

ROOF, PILLAR, AND WALL BLOCKS

NEW TEMPLE SITE

and, almost at once, trouble broke out. During the reign of his son Merenptah, the Egyptians faced a new menace from the north. Libyans from the western desert allied with Mediterranean freebooters to attack Egypt, and thirty years later, soon after 1200 BC, a further and more dangerous wave of invaders threatened the country. The attack was repulsed by the third Ramesses, but the effort, combined with internal anarchy and economic decline, weakened Egyptian control over Nubia. The descendants of Ramesses, many of whom bore his name, still did a little building but the country slipped gradually from their hands.

One monument survives from this troubled time to show that Nubia was still under Egypt's rule. In a cliff not far from the river at Aniba, one of Mi'am's citizens hewed himself out a tomb. Pennut, in spite of his Egyptian name, was another of those native Nubians who rose in favour with the Pharaoh and acquired wealth and local importance. He had, it seems, dedicated in the temple of Aniba a statue of Ramesses VI at his own expense. The scenes sculptured round the walls of the tomb, in good Egyptian style, show him presented with two silver vases and a robe of state. Other reliefs depict the dead man and his wife in the presence of the gods of the underworld.

By 1000 BC, if not earlier, Nubia must have regained her independence, but this is mere conjecture, for there is no mention of the country in the sparse records of the period in Egypt, and scarcely any archaeological remains in Nubia can be dated to this period: presumably the area was severely depopulated, though what may have been the reason we do not know. For more than two hundred and fifty years, the history of Nubia is a blank.

CHAPTER VI
Kings of Napata and Meroe

About 750 BC a remarkable family came into power in the south, who were to turn Kush for a short time into a world power. They were, it seems, chieftains of the district of Napata, near the remarkable flat-topped hill known as the Gebel Barkal, which had been an administrative centre in the New Kingdom and a centre of the worship of the sun-god, Amon-Rê. When they enter the light of history, they appear to have been thoroughly Egyptianized. Worshippers of the gods of Egypt, they are depicted in Egyptian dress and they buried their dead much as the Egyptians did, with rites of mummification, and in pyramids. The development of their tombs, from simple mounds to sophisticated stone-built pyramids with subterranean chambers, has made it possible for a chronological sequence to be worked out, and it has been assumed that the family must go back to the ninth century BC. Were they then Egyptians who had fled south from Thebes at some time of trouble, perhaps at the end of the New Kingdom when the country was split by civil war? Were they Libyans from the western oases? Or were they native African chieftains, who had adopted the civilization of their masters at a time when Nubia was still governed by the Egyptian viceroys? No certain answer has been found. The first warning that the Egyptians themselves seem to have had was the sudden arrival of Piankhy, son of Kashta, in Thebes in 730 BC; one by one the cities of the Nile Valley succumbed to his army; Hermopolis was starved out, and Memphis stormed; one by one the Delta cities capitulated and Piankhy found himself master of Egypt. He was followed by a succession of warrior kings no less remarkable.

The Kushite Dynasty is the twenty-fifth in Manetho's list of the kings of Egypt. The capital of Kush was still Napata but the kings were crowned at Memphis and spent much of their time in Egypt; in their admiration for the Egyptian way of life they encouraged artists and craftsmen and ruled competently. Prosperity, by now at a low ebb, began to revive and trade flourished. The Kushite kings even aspired to win the ancient prestige of the imperial pharaohs of the New Kingdom, carrying their arms into Syria and by doing so, challenging the mighty Assyrian empire in a bid to win supremacy in western Asia. King Taharqa, whose portraits show him as a bull-necked powerful man with negroid features, started his reign well. In the year of his accession, 688 BC, there were exceptionally heavy rains in Nubia, 'so that the hills glistened'. The high Nile flood which resulted, destroyed rats and other vermin and produced a bumper harvest. These were good omens, and they were recorded on stelae (memorial stones) set up in various Egyptian and Nubian cities. From his capital at Tanis, in the eastern Delta, he sent envoys to the Kings of Tyre and Sidon and to Hezekiah, King of Judah, urging them to throw off the Assyrian yoke, and promising aid. The revolt failed, and Assyrian vengeance was not long delayed: Esarhaddon, King of Assyria, marched against 'Tarku, King of Egypt and Kush', and after several battles, drove him back to Memphis, which Esarhaddon then captured and burnt. Driving the Kushites out of Egypt, he set up Egyptian governors as vassals of Assyria in the various provinces. Their tenure of office was brief, however, for on Esarhaddon's death, Taharqa returned and was able to regain possession of Memphis.

His triumph, too, was short-lived. Ashur-bani-pal, the last great king of Assyria, swooped down and Taharqa was again driven from Memphis. This was Taharqa's last attempt, but his son and successor, Tanutamen, emboldened by a dream of two cobras which his soothsayers interpreted as a sign that he, too, would wear the double crown, defied Assyria once more and threw out the Memphite garrison. This time there was no quarter. In 656 BC Thebes was sacked, the whole of Egypt annexed by Ashur-bani-pal, and Tanutamen fled back to Napata, never to reappear. After less than seventy-five years, the Kushite years, the Kushite adventure was at an end.

The kings of Napata showed little interest in Lower Nubia except as a corridor leading to Egypt. Their building activities were centred in Egypt itself and in the Kushite homeland, where at Gem-Aton (now Kawa), and Napata the capital, they raised temples to the sun-god, Amon-Rê. The great temple of this god at Gebel Barkal, in size second only to that of Karnak, was greatly enlarged and adorned; fragments of statues subsequently smashed were of excellent Egyptian workmasnhip and indeed Taharqa himself states, on one of the stelae which he set up in the temple at Kawa, that he brought craftsmen from Memphis to work on the reliefs and furnishings. The royal burials of the Dynasty, at Kurru and Nuri, not far from Napata, tend to conform with Egyptian funerary practice, but they differ in significant details.

Instead of lying stiffly on their backs in coffins, the mummies were laid on their sides on beds or couches, as if sleeping. The Kushite pyramids were more slender and pointed than Egyptian pyramids; moreover, some of the Kushite kings had their favourite horses, four to a chariot team, buried near them, upright and still in their silver harness – a barbaric custom which we shall meet again (p. 65).

THE KINGDOM OF MEROE

Though the Kushite kings, after Tanutamen's rout, did not again venture to set foot in Egypt, they continued to give themselves the old title of the Pharaohs, 'King of Upper and Lower Egypt'. This fiction was kept up even when, some time in the sixth century BC, the capital was moved south to Meroe, between the Fifth and Sixth Cataracts, a little above the confluence of the Rivers Nile and Atbara. It is possible that the move was made for strategic reasons, for the Pharaoh, Psammetichus II, in 591 BC sent an army upstream from Egypt and penetrated far into Kushite territory, probably sacking Napata. His mercenaries, among whom there were Greeks and Carians from Asia Minor, stopped at Abu Simbel on the way, and on the leg of one of the colossal figures in front of the temple, at which they must have gazed in wonder, they carved an inscription in Greek recording the names of their leaders. The inscription, incidentally, is of great interest to classical scholars, for it happens to be one of the earliest known specimens of archaic Greek writing.

Henceforward, the Meroitic civilization, as it is called, developed along its own lines, ever more cut off from Egypt, though contact by trade along the Nile Valley continued. The Greeks knew of the kingdom of Meroe, though they seldom visited it. They called it Ethiopia, the 'Land of the Burnt-Faces'. (In the same way, the name Sudan stands for the Arabic Bilad es-Sudan, the 'Lands of the Blacks'.) In the old days, historians used to refer to the Kushite dynasty of Napata as the Ethiopian dynasty, but this was unfortunate since it led to confusion with the land which is nowadays called Ethiopia – the kingdom of Abyssinia. Not very much is known about the history of Meroe and the very names and order of kings are in dispute. There is no king-list, such as those which guide us through Egyptian history, and the length of reign of each king can only be estimated from the size and richness of the burial and its location. The position of Meroe, in a fertile stretch of the Nile and with access to important sources of iron, brought prosperity to the Meroitic kings. They traded along the Red Sea coast and had access to the markets of Central Africa. Their rule lasted until about AD 350, when Meroe was finally destroyed by their rivals, the Axumites of Abyssinia.

At first, the Egyptian hieroglyphic script and language were used in inscriptions, and these can, of course, be read, but the use of them became increasingly inept. A change came in the second century BC: a limited number of the hieroglyphs were thenceforward employed to form a kind of alphabet in which to write another language, presumably the native Meriotic tongue. A cursive linear script gradually developed for greater ease of writing. Unfortunately, though Meroitic inscriptions can be read, the language is not yet well understood; it appears to have no affinity with any of the many modern African languages and there are no bilingual inscriptions to help the would-be historian of Meroe.

Meroitic inscriptions occur in some quantity in Nubia and the characteristic, strikingly painted pottery is found in cemeteries and settlements. These date for the most part to the later period of Meroitic history, for the Dodekaschoinos, the name given by the Greeks to Lower Nubia, the Twelve *Schoinoi* (furlongs), was regarded as within the realm of the first Egyptian Ptolemies. In the last centuries BC, the Ptolemaic kings built temples at Philae, Kalabsha and Qertassi; their authority reached as far south as Hierasykamínos (el-Maharraqa). This gave them control of the Wady Allaki gold mines. The names of Meroitic kings and Ptolemies occur together on some temples, however, and it was the Meroitic King Ergamenes (Arqamani) who built the temple of Dakka, in which Ptolemy IV also appears as co-founder; Arqamani's name is also inscribed in the temple of Philae on the border of Egypt; this fact, and similar evidence of co-operation in the early second century at Dabod, indicates that relations between Egypt and Meroe were at least intermittently friendly. Not until the Roman legions took over Egypt was there war: Strabo's account of the battle at Dakka describes the rout of 'Queen Candace, who was ruler of the Ethiopians in my time – a masculine sort of woman, and blind in one eye'. Women of the royal family had great importance in Meroe, and Candace seems to have been a kind of royal title given to the Queen.

Lower Nubia now became a centre of trade; large settlements grew up in the northern part of the country, under Ptolemaic patronage, and the population of Meroitic Nubia increased, judging by the number of cemeteries and settlements.

At Qasr Ibrim there is a stone building which may be a Meroitic temple; it is unfortunately uninscribed, but over the doorway to the fortress is a lintel with a winged disc which may have come from the temple. Symbols of the gods derived from Egyptian iconography, but often strangely misunderstood and altered in the copying, are usual decorations of objects of stone or bronze in the Meroitic cemetery at Ibrim and the large cemeteries at Karanog and Faras. Little is known of Meroitic religion, but it clearly derives its inspiration from the religion of ancient Egypt. Local gods were given Egyptian dress and attributes, but betray their African nature by being lion-headed or, like the god Apedemak at Naga, having multiple arms and heads, perhaps under Indian influence. Offering tables of Egyptian type were common in the Meroitic graves of Nubia, and on some of them had been placed the rather quaint stone figure of a human-headed bird, the Egyptian concept of the *Ba*, or soul.

ON THE SUMMIT OF QASR IBRÎM. The stone building on the edge of the escarpment is undecorated and has an unfinished appearance. It may have been a Meroitic temple. Far below, the tops of trees can be seen sticking out of the water: it is winter, and the Nile, held back farther north by the old dam, is already flooding the valley.

CHAPTER VII
Nubia in Roman Times

In 30 BC, after the Battle of Actium, Egypt became a province of Rome, and so, in theory at least, did the Dodekaschoinos. The interest of the occupying power, however, lay rather in the rich agricultural lands north of Aswan, rather than in the poor south, and the activities of their armies had more to do with keeping the peace and ensuring the security of their subjects north of the First Cataract than with attempting to occupy and govern their most southerly possession. Emboldened by the fall of the last of the Ptolemies, the Kushites of Meroe seized Premnis (Qasr Ibrim), descended upon Philae and Elephantine, and wrecked temples, wrenching the bronze statues of Augustus from their pedestals and carrying them off to Meroe. Retaliation was swift: a Roman army led by the general Gaius Petronius marched south in 23 BC, defeated the Kushite queen, Candace, at Pselkis (Dakka) and reoccupied Ibrim, turning it into a garrison town. Strabo describes the rout at Pselkis: 'Some were herded into the city, some took refuge on an island nearby, plunging in and swimming across the strait, for the crocodiles here were not very numerous by reason of the current.' The fleeing army was pursued as far as Napata. Qasr Ibrim was refortified by the Romans and became the frontier.

Henceforward an uneasy peace was kept with the Kushites. The Emperor Nero appears to have contemplated the conquest of Meroe, for he sent a handful of men on an expedition to the heart of the kingdom to spy out the land; the report which they brought back to Rome shows that they must have penetrated into equatorial Africa, but they gave it as their opinion that the country was too remote and poor to be worth the trouble of conquering.

Under Roman rule Lower Nubia seems to have regained a little of her prosperity for a time, and a few temples were built, the most southerly at Maharraqa, the limit of the Dodekaschoinos. Like the Ptolemies, the Roman emperors regarded themselves as the heirs of the Pharaohs, and as a matter of policy they encouraged the dogma that they, too, were gods incarnate. In the temples which they built to the honour of the gods in Egypt and Nubia, they are depicted in the trappings of godhead, and it was thought perfectly natural that the emperors Trajan, Hadrian and Caligula should appear dressed in

QASR IBRÎM: THE FORTRESS ON THE ROCK. A road winds up to the gateway. The massive walls, many times repaired, fringe the edge of the rock. Ibrim was a stronghold in the eighteenth dynasty (sixteenth century BC) and thenceforward played a significant role in Nubian history through Meroitic to Christian and Islamic times.

the short tunic and double crown, offering incense to Amon-Rê, Ptah, Hathor and the other deities of the Egyptian pantheon.

With the exception of Abu Simbel, Kalabsha is the best preserved temple in Nubia. Here at Talmis, as the place was called, the Emperor Augustus built a large stone temple to the local lion-headed god Mandulis, on the foundations of a New Kingdom shrine. It was further embellished by Caligula and Trajan. The approach from the river was by a broad balustraded causeway a hundred feet long, leading to a platform or podium in front of the pylon gateway. On the farther wall of the courtyard within the gateway, and on the screen wall dividing the pillared hall beyond from the inner halls and sanctuary, are reliefs depicting the Pharaoh-Emperor making offerings to the gods; all the figures were gaily painted (a fact which must be remembered when looking at Egyptian temples) and traces of paint still remain. This fine temple has been taken down, stone by stone, by a team of engineers and architects from West Germany, and re-erected twenty-seven miles farther north on an elevated site overlooking the High Dam, where it is visited by many hundreds of tourists every year. Nearby has been placed the small temple of Beit al Wali (see above, p. 44) and, also in the vicinity, the graceful Ptolemaic 'kiosk' from Qertassi has been set on an eminence looking out over Lake Nasser.

Soon the Romans faced fresh dangers from the Nubian desert, by the arrival of a nation of fierce camel-riding nomads known to them as the Blemmyes, who may be the ancestors of the Sudanese Beja-people. Their religion and customs, probably influenced by contact with the Kushites of Meroe, were a source for disapproving comment by the Byzantine writer Procopius, who ascribes to them the practice of human sacrifice. They were greatly feared by the settled population of the Nile Valley and their raids extended north of the First Cataract into the Thebaid. Yet another nomadic people, called the Nobatae or Nobatians, lived in the Nubian desert west of the Nile and these, too, raided the Dodekaschoinos and kept the small Roman army of occupation busy. Sometimes they came into conflict with the Blemmyes, to whom they may have been distantly related. At other times the two nations made common cause against the Romans and together attacked the frontier. Gradually Rome's hold on Nubia loosened; the Emperor Diocletian recalled his garrisons and the frontier was set at Syene (Aswan). Although by now Egypt was becoming a Christian country, the old pagan gods were still worshipped in Nubia and both Nobatae and Blemmyes held in reverence a goddess whom they identified with Isis the Great Mother; her temple at Philae was a place of pilgrimage for them. In AD 453 a Roman army was sent on a punitive expedition to put an end, once and for all, to the nomads' incursions, and they were forced to agree to keep the peace for a hundred years; by the terms of the treaty both peoples were to be allowed an annual visit to Philae, and they might from time to time borrow the statue of the goddess. The cult of Isis had gained great popularity in Ptolemaic and Roman Egypt and her devotees were even to be found in Rome itself. The poignant myth of the death of Osiris, his mourning wife's search for his body and his eventual resurrection, had many different forms; the figure of Isis as wife and mother had a universal appeal and her statues were credited with healing powers.

The temple of Isis is the largest of the graceful buildings of Ptolemaic and

Roman date which crown the small island of Philae, above the First Cataract. With its lush vegetation and waving palms, and its great pillars with their spreading flower capitals, Philae was once known to tourists as the Pearl of Egypt; but this was before the raising of the Aswan Dam. Situated upstream in the middle of the lake formed by the dam, the temples have every year been submerged by the water to such an extent that when the Nile is high, for most of the winter and spring, nothing has been seen of them except two oblongs of stone, the tops of the high pylons of the temple of Isis, and a red buoy which marks the whereabouts of the graceful kiosk known as 'Pharaoh's Bed'. The preservation of Philae posed an especial problem and its fate was long in the balance, for its very existence became threatened. With the erection of the High Dam, the island and its temples were caught in a swirl of water between the old dam and the new, and the water level fluctuated daily with the opening and closing of the sluices controlling the flow of water through the turbines for hydro-electric power. If no action were taken, the strong currents would soon eat away the stone and bring down the temples. There were two alternatives here: either to move the whole complex of temples to another site, or to enclose the island in a ring of dykes and so form a low-level 'lake-within-a-lake', in such a way that visitors would once more be able to see the famous beauty-spot in its proper setting of water and trees. In May 1968 the decision was finally taken to dismantle the temples and re-erect them on a nearby island, permanently above the Nile's high-water mark. If the needed twelve million dollars can be raised – and the government of the United Arab Republic has promised to contribute one-third of this sum – the future of this, the last and loveliest of the monuments of Nubia, will at last be ensured.

The introduction into Nubia during the first century AD of the water-wheel turned by animals greatly improved agricultural production, and areas never before cultivated could be brought under the plough. The population of Nubia seems to have been larger at this time than ever it had been before, perhaps three times as much as it had been at the height of its prosperity during the New Kingdom. Trade flourished between the Romans and the Meroites and the influence of classical motifs is seen on pottery from the south. Meroitic Nubia, too, enjoyed an era of prosperity. Houses of the period were substantial structures with thick walls, often roofed with barrel vaulting; some had many rooms grouped around open courts. At Karanog, north of

Abu Simbel, a mudbrick building three stories high combined the character of fortress and palace; it must have been the residence of a local governor. Other large rambling buildings at other sites may possibly have housed a number of families together.

KINGS OF THE 'X-GROUP'

When the Aswan Dam was raised for the second time in 1927, two Englishmen, W. B. Emery, and his assistant L. Kirwan, were exploring the area about to be flooded on either side of the Nile. South of Abu Simbel, a group of curious conical mounds at Ballana and, on the opposite bank, at Qostol, caught their eye and they decided to make a trial excavation. The first day's digging met with an encouraging reward: crawling on hands and knees down a passage cut by robbers in one of the Qostol mounds, the excavators found themselves gazing through a hole into a low tomb-vault filled with pottery, fragments of wood and human bones in confusion. Further exploration showed that the mound covered a complex of underground chambers in which an evidently important personage had been buried with provisions for the next world; a number of other human bodies accompanied him; these people, together with his horses, silver-mounted saddles and silver bridles and collars hung with bells, and also his camels and his donkeys, had all been poleaxed and also buried to keep him company and serve him in the next world.

Further mounds were examined, with similar result, and eventually, at Ballana, the tumulus-graves of kings themselves were found. They were tall men, with negroid features, and they lay on wooden biers, with jewel-encrusted crowns on their head, their spears and swords at their sides. With them were their queens, also wearing crowns and decked with jewellery. Other bodies were presumably of members of the family, and in each tomb there were large numbers of male and female slaves. Some of these lay as if they had been felled from behind with a club, others appeared to have been strangled. It is not difficult to imagine the horror of that day of burial and massacre, when the wretched victims were dragged down the ramp to accompany their master to the grave. Even the king's dogs had been killed. The funerary equipment buried in these royal tombs was rich and excellently preserved in the dry sand. There were vessels of silver and bronze, boxes of wood with carved panels, iron weapons with silver mounts, leather quivers

THE FUNERAL OF A WARRIOR KING OF THE 'X-GROUP' was accompanied by grim rites. Here an attempt has been made to recreate the scene. Horses and camels are being driven down the ramp; they and their grooms and countless slaves will be slaughtered to accompany the chieftain to the next world. Over the tomb, the survivors will heap a huge mound of earth to protect the burial and its treasures.

and shields, and a gaming board with ivory and ebony pieces, together with a cheat-proof dicebox of ingenious design. Necklaces and bracelets were encrusted with beryls, amethysts and garnets, carnelian, crystal and jasper; a few were of gold. Many of the decorative motifs were of Meroitic origin: among the strange emblems of deities, for instance, was a composite figure of a recumbent god with a hawk's head, the body of a lion and a crocodile's tail, holding a branch with human hands . . . a figure which is exactly paralleled in the Meroitic south. Many objects, on the other hand, showed Byzantine influence and some of the lamps and incense burners appeared to be imports from the Hellenistic world, perhaps the work of Alexandrian craftsmen. One or two of these could be dated by style, or by their hall-mark, to the fifth or sixth century A D, but a coin found in one tomb was of the Roman Emperor Valens (A D 364–378) and it is probable that the burials spanned something like three centuries.

Who were these people? There were no inscriptions in their tombs, only a few words of Meroitic and a little Greek. Cemeteries containing similar grave-goods have been found on other sites, notably at Qasr Ibrim in the low desert around the foot of the rock, at Gemai and Firka near the Second Cataract, and at Wawa near the Third. Excavators have labelled them the X-Group, and still hesitate to identify them with one or other of the peoples mentioned by classical authors as having lived in Nubia at this time. One opinion holds them to be the Blemmyes. But the historian Olympiodorus gives us a clue. When he visited Lower Nubia in AD 421 he found the Blemmyes in occupation of former Roman territory north of Ibrim, with their capital at Kalabsha. Now an inscription of Silko, King of the Nobatae, in the temple of Kalabsha records in bombastic language how he defeated the Blemmyes and drove them out. The inscription is dated by its style of calligraphy to the fifth century. Until then the Nobatae must have lived farther south, beyond Ibrim . . . and this is precisely where the royal tombs of the X-Group are. It is probable then that in the X-Group we must recognize the Nobatian rulers of Nubia; the manner of their burial bears witness to their wealth and importance, the barbaric splendour and the savagery of their lives.

GEBEL ADDA: THE FORT ON THE HILLTOP. Medieval buildings crown the hill and cemeteries of all periods surround the stronghold. A combined expedition from the Universities of Alexandria, Yale and Pennsylvania was responsible for its excavation.

CHAPTER VIII
The Cross and the Crescent

Christianity came comparatively late to Nubia. In Egypt there were almost certainly Christian converts late in the first century and the earliest known Christian manuscript, a scrap of papyrus containing part of a codex of the Gospel of St John, is dated to the early part of the second century. By the end of that century, Christianity was widespread in Upper Egypt as well as in Alexandria and the Delta, and Bishop Clement of Alexandria could write in about AD 200 that the faith had spread 'to every nation, village and town'. It is probable that at this time there were secret converts in Nubia, too; although the country continued to be a stronghold of the old, polytheistic religion, hermit's cells found in Nubia suggest that the ascetic movement had spread south of the First Cataract.

The earliest missionaries were Greek-speaking, and therefore prosyletized among the Hellenized Egyptians and Greeks living in Egypt. But the new religion with its promise of life after death had an especial appeal also for the native Egyptians, accustomed as they were to the expectation of life beyond the grave in the realm of the god Osiris. Many converts to Christianity indeed continued to mummify their dead and to bury furniture, implements and even food and drink in the graves to sustain their relatives in the next world. Only the presence of the cross, or that form of it known as the *crux ansata*, derived from the pagan hieroglyphic sign meaning 'life', distinguishes some of the early Christian burials in Egypt and Nubia from those of their pagan contemporaries.

In the reign of Constantine the Great, who became sole Emperor in AD 324, Christianity became the official religion of the Roman Empire, and from the middle of the fourth century, Egypt was essentially a Christian country. The kingdom of Ethiopia was converted about AD 350, but Nubia was not formally Christianized until, in AD 543, the first missionaries were sent from Byzantium by the Emperor Justinian to the court of the king of the Nobatae. Schism at this time was rending the Byzantine church, and in Egypt the so-called Monophysite heresy had been officially adopted. Its adherents maintained that in the person of Christ there was only one nature,

68

not many natures. Justinian's missionaries were naturally of the Orthodox (or Melkite) faith of Byzantium, and Nubia might thenceforward have been converted to Orthodoxy had it not been for the intrigues of the Empress Theodora, Justinian's remarkable wife, who herself favoured the Monophysites. She sent her own envoy, Julian, hotfoot after those of her husband, and he succeeded in persuading the governor of the district of Thebes to arrest the Melkite mission. The king of the Nobatae was converted by Julian, and his subjects followed his lead.

Henceforward Monophysite Christianity flourished in Nubia. Monasteries proliferated. The Nobatian king, Mercourios, the 'new Constantine', as he was called, encouraged the people to turn their temples into churches. Most of the Pharaonic temples of Nubia still show signs of their transformation: walls were plastered or whitewashed to obliterate the sculptured figures of the old gods and to provide a surface for mural paintings depicting Biblical

CHRISTIAN SEBU'A. From the court of the temple of Ramesses II a ramp led up to the Christian church into which the interior was converted. Whitewash, and paintings of saints and angels, concealed the pagan gods on the walls. The heads of the colossal figures in the courtyard were struck off.

scenes, angels, saints and patriarchs of the church. At Beit al Wali, domes were constructed and the inner court was turned into the nave of the church; at Wady es Sebu'a the Osirid statues in the hypostyle hall were dismantled and a brick apse and altar built. In the sanctuary, where figures of Ramesses II had originally stood on either side, offering bunches of lotus blossoms to four deities, the seated gods were chiselled out to make a flat surface for a fresco depicting St Peter with a large key. The whitewash has now been removed from the side reliefs, creating the odd illusion that the Pharaoh is offering his bouquets to the saint.

From the beginning of the seventh century onwards, the Nubian church was put under the charge of a metropolitan bishop appointed by the Patriarch of Alexandria. His residence was in Pachoras, the modern Faras, south of Abu Simbel and just north of Wady Halfa, not far from the modern border between Egypt and the Sudan, a town which was probably also the capital of Nobatia. Here ruins of a number of monasteries and churches have been excavated, the most remarkable and largest being that uncovered between 1961 and 1963 by a Polish expedition from the University of Warsaw. On the site of a smaller church destroyed by the Muslims in one of their early raids, a building arose which must have been the Cathedral of Faras. This church has yielded some of the most remarkable and most unexpected treasures that have come to light during the recent campaign sponsored by UNESCO. The building, completed by the fifth bishop, Paulos, in AD 707, was of stone and mudbrick; on the walls the excavators found layer upon layer of wall-paintings, a remarkable series constituting a unique museum of Byzantine art and iconography.

Each bishop, on his consecration, had himself depicted on the walls of the church; the gravely-staring visages of the later ones are painted dark brown, in contrast with the white-faced angel or saint who protects them; these were Nubians of the locality, not envoys from the north. A list of twenty-seven metropolitan bishops between AD 870 and 999 enables the tombs disposed around the church to be placed in their historical sequence. Each bishop, too, added fresh decoration to the walls for the adornment of the church and the instruction of his flock . . . for these paintings served as text-books to the illiterate. A large painting of the ninth century, for instance, depicts Christ in glory surrounded by his angels; another shows Shadrach, Meshach and Abednego being delivered from the Burning Fiery Furnace.

70

The painting is in a remarkable state of preservation, the colours still fresh though the surface of the plaster is a little pitted. It extends over the wall on the south side of the church. In the background, orange-red flames outline the figures. The great figure of the archangel occupies the centre of the composition; he is dressed in a long white robe and mantle and brown pointed shoes, and he wears a crown set with precious stones. Behind his head is a halo of yellow. His face is gently smiling, his eyebrows arched. His outstretched wings are strewn with peacock's tail-feathers. He holds in his hand a round fluted paten, or sacramental dish, and in his right hand, supported by his left, is the long staff, tipped with a cross, with which he makes a gesture of protection in front of the three Hebrews. These are dressed in tea-cosy hats, long close-fitting trousers and tunics girded at the waist, bordered with an elaborate design representing an embroidery of precious stones and pearls. Over their shoulders are dark-blue cloaks, also bejewelled, and bracelets and collars set with gems. Each holds up his hands in supplication, two on the right of the angel and one on his left. They are named Ananias, Azarias and Misael, the original names of the three 'children of Judah' who, with Daniel, were given Babylonian nicknames and achieved high honour at court; their rich apparel proclaims their rank. In the 'Book of Daniel' they are described as having been cast into the furnace in 'their coats, their hose and their hats'. The subject was a favourite one among the early Christians, and versions of the scene have been found in several Nubian churches. It is interesting that in this church the archangel Michael plays a leading part and takes over the role of the mysterious fourth figure walking in the fire, whose 'form is like the Son of God'.

A little later in date, perhaps the very end of the tenth century, is another large scene, that of the Nativity, with the Virgin Mary reclining on a splendid couch, surrounded by angels swinging censers, while ass and ox guard the Child in his crib above. Two brown-skinned shepherds come running with their staves and water-bottles and the three Magi gallop on splendidly caparisoned horses, holding their gifts aloft. The composition has a vigour and spontaneity that places it among the finest extant examples of provincial Byzantine art. Many other paintings of almost equal merit date from the early years of the eleventh century.

Such treasures had to be saved at all costs. The mud churches themselves would drown and dissolve when the waters rose, and the problem of the

MURAL PAINTING FROM THE CATHEDRAL CHURCH AT FARAS. The Nativity is pictured. The Virgin Mary reclining on a couch is the central figure. The church long remained roofless and in ruins, but drift sand protected the fresh colour of the frescoes.

murals taxed the ingenuity and patience of the experts. The method most generally employed has been to coat the friable painted plaster surface with plastic glue and to paste over it layer upon layer of gauze, strengthened with strips of linen. The plaster face could then be cut away from the wall, removed and mounted on a frame of wood or fibreglass. In the laboratory the gauze could be carefully peeled off with the aid of a wet cloth, to reveal the colours still bright beneath, and the surface could then be consolidated and restored for re-mounting on a wall. A more difficult task was the removal of successive paintings where layers of different dates lay one on top of another. Many of the frescoes from Faras have now been successfully transplanted and some are on display in the Museum at Khartoum, while others are in Warsaw. Other mural paintings, some of comparable merit, were found in the church of Abdullah Nikri, and a Dutch expedition has successfully 'lifted' many of these. It will now be possible to write a new chapter into the history of

72

Byzantine art.

It may have been Bishop Yoannes (997–1005), or his successor the black-bearded Bishop Marianos, who introduced the Melkite (or Orthodox) doctrine into Nubia; henceforward relations between the church in Nubia and the Monophysite Coptic Christians in Egypt became estranged. At about the same time the Christian kings of the south began to adopt a more aggressive policy towards their Muslim neighbours. Egypt had been conquered by the General, Amr ibn el Âs, in AD 640; ever since that time, the kingdom of Nubia had faced the constant threat of an Arab invasion. In 642 Emir Abdullah ibn Sa'ad led an army south to the Dongola reach above the

TEMPLE INTO CHURCH AT ABU ODA. This small shrine to the south of Abu Simbel was carved in the rock by Horemheb, last king of the eighteenth dynasty. A large figure of Christ has been painted on the ceiling. Saints and angels and Byzantine decorative motifs cover the walls.

Third Cataract, but the town of Dongola held out against the catapults of Islam, and a treaty was signed which lasted for some six hundred years. By its terms, the Aswan frontier was guaranteed. 'Ye people of Nubia, ye shall dwell in safety under the safeguard of God and his apostle, Muhammad the prophet (whom God bless and save). We will not attack you, nor wage war on you, nor make incursions against you, so long as ye abide by the terms settled between us and you. When ye enter our country it shall be but as travellers, not settlers . . . ye shall take care of the mosque which the Muslims have built in the outskirts of your city, and hinder none from praying there; ye shall clean it, light it and honour it. Every year ye shall pay 360 head of slaves to the Leader of the Muslims . . . without bodily defects, males and females, but no old men nor old women nor young children. Ye shall deliver them to the Governor of Aswan. . . . If ye harbour a Muslim slave, or kill a Muslim or an ally, or attempt to destroy the mosque which the Muslims have built on the outskirts of your city, or withhold any of the 360 slaves, then this promised peace and security will be withdrawn from you, and we shall revert to hostility, until Allah decide between us, and He is the best of Umpires.' In return for this grim payment of human tribute, a handsome present of wheat, foodstuffs, cloth and horses was made by the Arabs to the Nubians.

MUSLIM TOMBS AT GEBEL ADDA. In the desert behind the fortified town on Gebel Adda (see p. 67) there were dozens of these small cupolas. The cemetery also contained graves of earlier periods.

SABAGURA. This Christian town, on the east bank of the Nile opposite Gerf Husein, has been excavated by the University of Milan. The mudbrick vaults and walls of houses still stand to a considerable height. The town was strongly walled.

Henceforward trade flourished. Recent excavation of town and village sites such as that at Arminna, has provided material evidence that in the centuries between AD 850 and AD 1100, in what the American excavators named the Classic Christian period, there were frequent importations of wine in amphorae from the monasteries of Egypt and also an interchange of goods between Nubia and the farther Sudan, resulting in considerable prosperity. Some of the houses of this period are well built and have seven or eight rooms.

In the twelfth century, as a result of a rebellion of the Nubians, who had ravaged Aswan and raided Upper Egypt, a punitive expedition was sent by Salahuddin, the celebrated Saladin, Sultan of Syria and Egypt, and best known to the West as the conqueror of Richard I in the third Crusade. Qasr Ibrim, the fortress on the rock, was captured by Saladin's brother, Shams el-Dowlah, and the bishop was tortured; many prisoners were taken and hundreds of pigs killed by the pork-abhorring Muslims. Ibrim remained for a time a Muslim stronghold but Faras appears to have escaped un-

75

scathed, and enjoyed its greatest prosperity in the mid-twelfth century, judging by the number of murals in the cathedral and their technical excellence.

But the Muslims again attacked, using Ibrim as their base, and swept south; at the Battle of Adindan, near Faras, their leader was killed, but Faras was captured and destroyed. The roof of the nave of the cathedral collapsed and was never replaced, and the cathedral itself was gradually abandoned. Though the Muslims withdrew, the history of Christianity in Nubia was nearly at an end, and town settlements show signs of increasing impoverishment. The successors of the last bishop of Pachoras resided in Primis (Ibrim), though they still bore their old title. The burial place of some of these last bishops of the combined see of Primis and Pachoras have been found at Ibrim by Professor Plumley's expedition. One of these, still undisturbed when it was found in the crypt below the stone-built church, contained the body of

VAULTED CORRIDORS IN CHRISTIAN IKHMINDI. Mudbrick vaults sheltered the inhabitants from the fierce heat of the Nubian sun. In a square in the centre of the town stood a tiny church. The town was surrounded on three sides by massive fortification walls with buttress-towers, and was protected on the east by the river.

a prelate in full canonicals. Tucked among his robes were two paper scrolls, one written in Coptic and one in Arabic. When these were unrolled and read in the Museum in Cairo, they proved to be the dead man's deeds of consecration, giving the exact date, AD 1372. Other scrolls found at Ibrim confirm that Christianity still flourished in Nubia in the fourteenth century. Life must have been precarious for the Nubian Christians, however, for some of their towns have the appearance of strongholds built for defence, with high bastioned walls of stone. Sabagura is a striking example of such a town, and so is Ikhmindi; both of these are north of Ibrim and so in greater danger of attack from Egypt.

The ultimate fate of most of these Christian communities is not known, and the history of Nubia in the centuries that followed is extremely obscure. At the beginning of the sixteenth century the country was in so turbulent and lawless a condition that Sultan Selim sent a company of Bosnian mercenaries to restore order. They accomplished their task and established themselves in a garrison on a rock at Ibrim where, forgotten by their masters in Constantinople, they lived for more than three hundred years, intermarrying with the local population and turning the church into a mosque. The ruins of their roughly-built stone houses and narrow streets still cover the hill-top, and have to be cleared away to reach the older levels of occupation beneath. The last chapter at Ibrim was brief and bloody. At the beginning of the nineteenth century the Mamelukes, fleeing from the avenging army of the Khedive of Egypt, Mohammad Ali, occupied the fortress briefly, driving out the remnant of the Bosnians from their homes; but they were in in turn expelled by Mohammad Ali's son, Ismail Pasha; those that escaped the sword fled farther south. Thenceforward, Nubia and the Sudan came under the rule of Egypt.

Postscript

Inexorably, inch by inch, the waters rise in Nubia. The High Dam will be completed in 1970 and in a few years, Lake Nasser will have reached its full height. The waters already lap around the minaret of the mosque at Wady Halfa. Twenty-two temples have been dismantled and moved. Most of them have already been rebuilt on their new sites in Egypt and the Sudan. One small temple, as a return for aid given, is to go to New York, another to Holland; a third will be rebuilt in Italy. Some fifty countries have contributed, in one way or another, to the labour and expense of these operations, and the amount of their aid approaches twenty million dollars. The temples of Abu Simbel, rebuilt two hundred feet above their old site, were reopened to visitors in the autumn of 1968; an airstrip has been built and the site will eventually be accessible both by hydrofoil and by helicopter. Other temples

THE REBUILDING OF KALABSHA. A hilltop site is being prepared by German engineers for the re-erection of the temple. Blasting is in progress.

KALABSHA DISMANTLED. Cornice blocks belonging to the temple were carefully numbered before removal to a rocky eminence near the High Dam, where the temple has now been rebuilt.

are being grouped in new oases on the shore of the lake, one site overlooks the High Dam (Kalabsha, Beit al Wali and the charming little kiosk of Qertassi), another is near the former site of Wady es Sebu'a (Sebu'a and Dakka) and one in the Aniba district (Amada and the tomb of Pennut). It is hoped that tourists will visit them, too, and that new villages will spring up, with trees and gardens and fields watered by the lake. There are plans to link Aswan by railway with Khartoum.

For the present, however, Nubia is emptied of its people. In 1963, some 52,000 Nubians from the Egyptian zone were moved north to Egypt, most of them to the region of Kom Ombo, twenty-five miles north of Aswan, where preparations had been made for their reception. On land reclaimed from the desert, a large area had been put under cultivation; here the Nubians have been given new houses and plots of land. Each newly-built village has its own mosque, primary school and clinic, and an attempt has been made to keep each community together in its new surroundings. A larger, central

79

NUBIAN HOUSES IN DABOD. The exterior walls are decorated with painted designs, and china bowls and plates have been let into the mud plaster. The scarecrow on the wall was said to scare away wolves from the village and protect the hencoops inside.

town called Nasser City has a hospital and a secondary school. A sugar factory processes the main crop, and cooperatives have been set up to help the newcomers to adapt to the new conditions.

Life for these people will be very different now. Nubia was a very poor country and most of the able-bodied men used to leave their homes to take service in Cairo as doorkeepers or domestic servants. The result was that the villages were largely populated by old men, women and children, and families were often separated for years. Little cultivation was possible, because, for most of the year, the fields were under water, and although supply boats brought oranges and dates, their diet was meagre and camels and donkeys lived on dried fodder and grew thin. Now, for the young, there are great prospects. They will benefit from the increased prosperity which the High Dam will bring to Egypt, and they will enjoy a far wider horizon of opportunity than ever they would have done in their former villages. But the old will look back, no doubt, with regret at the old way of life which is all that they have known: to the Nile without whose constant close companionship they will feel lost, to their spotlessly clean, gaily painted houses decorated with china saucers and painted patterns, to the steep winding alleys, and to the open courtyards of their Nubian homes.

In Sudanese Nubia there were sixty-five thousand people to re-settle. Their new homes are far away to the south near the Abyssinian border – at Khashm el Girba – where a dam has been built on the River Atbara to irrigate five hundred thousand acres of land. The evacuation from Wady Halfa was carried out in three stages, between 1963 and 1965. Around their new villages, sugar will again be the main crop, but industrial development is planned and the new dam will generate hydro-electric power.

The campaign to save the monuments of Nubia is almost at an end. Its results are now gradually being pieced together. The mass of information gained must be studied, digested and edited, and will become available through books and articles, on film and on microfilm.

THE ROCK TEMPLE OF DERR. Partly underwater for half the year since the last raising of the Aswan Dam, the temple has now been sawn piecemeal out of the rock and moved to a new site.

Inevitably, the campaign met with difficulties, and no one would claim that all its objectives have been achieved. Various obstacles had to be overcome. Archaeologists arrived in the region who had never before seen the Nile, were unacquainted with the methods of near eastern archaeology and could speak neither Arabic nor Nubian. Much had to be learned by trial and error. Not all expeditions were equally successful and not all completed the tasks allotted to them. There were unexpected discoveries; there were disappointments.

One thing is certain: the concept of the total study of an area in all its aspects has had novel consequences of great scientific importance. For the first time, a large area has been examined not only by archaeologists specializing in different periods of its history, but also by anthropologists, sociologists, economists and scientists in various fields, all combining to build up a complete and continuous picture of Nubia as it was, up to the moment when the waters rose to engulf it. In the past, for instance, excavation had concentrated largely upon cemeteries and upon temples and churches; a somewhat one-sided picture had, in consequence, been drawn, concerned largely with religious art and monumental architecture. Little was known of the daily life of the ancient Nubians, and little attention had been paid to their pottery and humbler artifacts, especially those of the late period. The excavation of stratified town and village sites has enabled a continuous graph to be made of the vicissitudes of these communities in terms of wealth or poverty, and of their contacts by trade. A 'corpus' or type-chart of pottery has been drawn up so that pots, or even potsherds of distinctive shape, can be assigned to their proper date and provenance. The most recent techniques have been brought to bear on the study of archaeological material and experience gained in quite different fields has often helped to shed light on what had long puzzled the Egyptologists.

In the history of this ancient land there are many problems still unsolved: a few of them have been outlined in this book. Some may find a solution when the final work of collation and publication is completed. Others may remain forever unanswered, for it is now too late.

INSIDE THE TEMPLE OF AMADA. The columns bear some resemblance to the Doric architecture of Greece, but they are a thousand years earlier. The reliefs were once brightly coloured, and traces of paint still remain.

Suggestions for further reading

A. J. Arkell — *A History of the Sudan to AD 1821*. 2nd edn. London, Athlone Press, 1961.

Amelia B. Edwards — *A Thousand Miles up the Nile*. London, Longmans Green, 1877.

W. B. Emery — *Egypt in Nubia*. London, Hutchinson, 1965.

W. B. Emery — *Nubian Treasure*. London, Methuen, 1948.

Walter A. Fairservis, Jr. — *The Ancient Kingdoms of the Nile*. Chicago, Mentor Books, 1962.

Max-Pol Fouchet — *Rescued Treasures of Egypt*. London, Geo. Allen & Unwin, 1965.

Sir Alan Gardiner — *Egypt of the Pharaohs*. Oxford, Clarendon Press, 1961.

Leslie Greener — *High Dam over Nubia*. London, Cassell, 1962.

F. Hinkel — *Tempel ziehen um*. Leipzig, Brockhaus, 1966.

Rex Keating — *Nubian Twilight*. London, Rupert Hart-Davis, 1962.

Hermann Kees — *Ancient Egypt: A Cultural Topography*. London, Faber & Faber, 1961.

Tom Little — *High Dam at Aswan*. London, Methuen. 1965.

Kasimiertz Michalowsky — *Faras: centre artistique de la Nubie chrétienne*. Leiden, Nederlands Instituut voor het Nabije Oosten, 1966.

T. Säve-Söderbergh — *Aegypten und Nubien*. Lund, Ohlsson, 1941.

P. L. Shinnie — *Meroe: A Civilization of the Sudan*. London, Thames & Hudson, 1968.

G. Steindorff and K. Seele — *When Egypt ruled the East*. Chicago, Phoenix Books, University of Chicago Press, 1942.

Bruce G. Trigger — History and Settlement in Lower Nubia (Yale University Publications in Anthropology 69). New Haven, Yale University, 1965.

A. E. P. Weigall — *Report on the Antiquities of Lower Nubia*. Oxford, Clarendon Press, 1907.

J. A. Wilson — *The Culture of Ancient Egypt*. Chicago, Phoenix Books. University of Chicago Press, 1956.

The periodical *Kush*, published annually by the Sudan Antiquities Service, contains excavation reports and articles of interest on the history and civilization of Nubia.

Index